RACISM
IN THE CHURCH

KILL THE
ROOT
DESTROY THE
TREE

KENNETH
COPELAND

KENNETH
COPELAND
PUBLICATIONS

Racism in the Church
Kill the Root, Destroy the Tree

ISBN 978-1-60463-325-2   30-0080

21 20 19 18 17 16   6 5 4 3 2 1

© 2016 Kenneth Copeland

Kenneth Copeland Publications
Fort Worth, TX 76192-0001

For more information about Kenneth Copeland Ministries, visit kcm.org or call 1-800-600-7395 (U.S. only) or +1-817-852-6000.

DEDICATION

I dedicate this book to my best friend, Gloria, who through her steadiness and lovingkindness, loved the strife and anger out of me. She and Jesus— what a love and healing team!

TABLE OF CONTENTS

CHAPTER 1

PUTTING THE SNAKE IN THE GRASS TO FLIGHT

For where envying and strife is, there is confusion and every evil work.

James 3:16

No one in their right mind would willingly turn a rattlesnake loose in their home. Yet people everywhere are doing it, right now. They're throwing open the doors of their lives to a spiritual snake so deadly that, according to the Bible, it brings with it "every evil work." They're making themselves vulnerable to a demonic enemy whose aim is to steal, kill and destroy, and whose strategy is to divide and conquer.

You can tell how well the strategy is working just by looking around. The results are clear for all to see: people fussing and fighting with each other, relationships rupturing, entire groups of people arguing, accusing and hating each other— over everything from government policy to race and religion.

As if that weren't bad enough, most of the people involved don't have the first clue as to why it's all happening. They can sense they're being threatened and wounded, but they're totally unaware of the snake in the grass. Determined to defend themselves, they're fighting with each other because they don't know who else to fight.

Even many born-again children of God have gotten caught up in the confusion. But, I'm writing this book because it's time for that to change. It's time for believers in Jesus to identify and go after the one who's actually *behind* all the strife and division. We're the only people who can do it. While others flounder helplessly in the face of this enemy, we've been equipped with the spiritual power to overcome him. We've been given the divine authority and ability to not only defend ourselves against this snake in the grass, but to rise up against him on behalf of others.

It's one of the first things Gloria and I learned when we started in the ministry many years ago. Spiritually, we didn't know very much back then. We certainly didn't have as much revelation as we do today. But we did understand this: "Where envying and strife is, there is confusion and every evil work" (James 3:16).

Even as spiritual beginners, we were smart enough to know we had absolutely no interest in giving the devil that kind of free rein in our lives. So, we sat down together at the kitchen table and made a quality decision. We agreed that strife and division were no longer an option for us and determined, before The LORD, to keep them out of our home and our ministry at all costs.

It's been nearly 50 years since we made that decision, and we've never once regretted it. On the contrary, we've become ever more grateful The LORD led us to make it because we've come to see how devastatingly destructive strife actually is. The WORD of God reveals it from Genesis to Revelation: Strife stops THE BLESSING of God and activates the curse—not only in our lives as individuals, but in entire churches, cities and nations.

Throughout history, whenever a major move of God has broken out on this planet, the devil has pushed people to divide up and start fighting each other. He's stirred up strife worldwide in an effort to stop the spread of the gospel and hinder the growth of the kingdom of God on earth. Wars, of one kind or another, have almost always accompanied the outpourings of God's glory—and these days, it's happening again.

In addition to cultural conflicts, threats of war and acts of terrorism and violence are practically a daily occurrence. They dominate the headlines and the 24/7 media cycle. And, the more they're reported, the bigger the problem grows.

Now, as in days gone by, the devil is doing the same old thing. (He doesn't have anything new.) Only this time, he's in a more desperate position than ever before. His time on this earth is running out (Revelation 12:12). Jesus is coming soon, and the Church has begun to step into the ultimate, end-time outpouring of God's glory.

I don't know how much evidence you've seen of it from where you're sitting, but I travel all over the world and can verify that a massive end-time harvest of souls is underway (Matthew 13:47-50). At this very moment, the gospel is being preached in places and among people the devil thought he had permanently locked up in spiritual darkness. God is doing supernatural, over-the-top things all across this planet. His Kingdom is on the move, and obviously, the devil is frantic to stop it!

It's really no wonder the world is in an uproar right now. These are biblical times. We've reached the last of the last days, and the events Jesus prophesied about in the Scriptures are happening. We're seeing unfold before our eyes the very things He warned His disciples about in Matthew 24, when they asked Him about the signs of the end of the age.

"Take heed that no man deceive you," He said. "For many shall come in my name, saying, I am Christ; and shall deceive many. And ye shall hear of wars and rumours of wars: see that ye be not troubled: for all these things must come to pass, but the end is not yet. For nation shall rise against nation, and kingdom against kingdom: and there shall be famines, and pestilences, and earthquakes, in divers places" (verses 4-7).

Notice, Jesus said in the last days *nation will rise against nation.* The Greek word translated *nation* is *ethnos.* It's a word that refers to ethnicities or races, groups of people who share the same skin color, nationality or way of thinking.

Let me ask you something: What do we call it today when people of one race or ethnicity rise up in hate against those of another race? We call it *racism,* don't we? But racism isn't really a Bible word. The Scriptures don't use it because from God's perspective, racism isn't a thing, it's a *spirit.* It's the spirit of division, the Greek word *dichostasia* indicates its work is "dissention, division and sedition."[1] It's a work of the devil himself and the demonic emissaries he sends out to do his divisionary work. By contrast, God's work is peace, unity, harmony and joy (John 14:27; Romans 14:17).

---

1 "division," *Strong's Exhaustive Concordance of the Bible,* (Nashville: Thomas Nelson, 1984) G1370.

The *spirit of division* is the enemy we're facing today, and those of us who are members of God's family need to become highly aware of it. We need to be constantly on guard against it because it's doing its best to set the world on fire all around us. It's working nonstop, not just to start race wars, and wars between nations, but to start wars between political parties, in communities, marriages and homes.

Worst of all, the spirit of division is targeting believers. It's trying to split up churches and separate members of the Body of Christ, knowing, even if we sometimes forget, that the saying, *United we stand, divided we fall,* is not just an old adage—it's spiritual law. As Jesus put it, "Every kingdom divided against itself is brought to desolation; and every city or house divided against itself shall not stand" (Matthew 12:25). Therefore, whatever the devil can divide, he can destroy.

Those of us who live in the United States of America, especially, need to wake up to this danger because spiritual unity is one of the truths on which this nation was founded. Even our Pledge of Allegiance declares that we are "one nation under God, *indivisible.*" Our very strength as a nation, and therefore our freedom, has always depended on our being undivided. Yet right now, Americans are picking sides and fighting each other with startling ferocity.

Democrats and Republicans have gone beyond just disagreeing and voting differently. Numbers of people in both political parties have gotten to the point where they actually hate the leaders of the opposing party. It's one thing when Americans disagree with a leader's decisions and to refuse to vote for him or her. But it's another thing when their disagreement turns to hatred. That's unnatural. Yet, it's happening.

I saw it during the previous presidential administration, and I'm seeing it again in the current administration. Some people are so angry with the president, they practically go berserk at the very mention of his name. They think their fury is politically driven, but it's not. It's spiritual. The door of government in America has been opened to the spirit of division, and the whole nation has suffered because of it.

Such suffering was never part of God's plan for this country. He never intended for Americans to divide up every chance they get and fight each other. His dream was always for this land to be a place where all cultures and people of all backgrounds could worship Him freely, together. He wanted a place where people weren't divided into all kinds of different, so-called "races."

As far as God is concerned, there are only two races on earth, anyway—those who have chosen to be a part of His family and those who haven't. From His perspective, the division between those two groups is the only division there is. He has never divided up mankind on the basis of money, clothing, culture, geography or skin color. People began listening to the devil and came up with those divisions. He got in there and started creating havoc.

That's what's happened in America. God's dream is for people of all colors—black, red, white, brown and yellow—to live and glorify Him together. If you doubt that, just look at heaven. Revelation 7:9-10 says what it will look like: "After this I beheld, and, lo, a great multitude, which no man could number, of all nations, and kindreds, and people, and tongues, stood before the throne, and before the Lamb, clothed with white robes, and palms in their hands; and cried with a loud voice, saying, Salvation to our God which sitteth upon the throne, and unto the Lamb."

God never intended for there to be enmity between people and races. He never meant for the black man to get to America in the belly of a slave ship! That's not God's way. He didn't intend for the red man to hang on to witchcraft and keep warring against each other's tribes. Nor did He want the white man to dominate and kill those who were here when he arrived.

His plan has always been BLESSING—people coming together through faith in Him and prospering together. This nation was built on the foundation of faith in the living God. He wanted to pour out His presence on His people who had dedicated this land to Him.[2] And He did His part to make it happen. He protected the first handful of settlers in remarkable ways, and has been protecting this nation ever since. We're the ones who have fouled things up. But in spite of all these things, this nation was dedicated to Him and, just as He has done with His people Israel, He will never give up on it. That's how He is. He'll stay with it…and stay with it, until His dream ultimately comes to pass.

Before Jesus comes and catches away the Church, I believe we'll come together and do what needs to be done. We'll pray and vote righteous people into authority who will deal with the spirit of division. We'll rise up in unity and elect leaders

---

"Cape Henry: the Beginning of a Christian Nation," Christian Broadcasting Network, http://www1.cbn.com/spirituallife/the-beginning-of-a-christian-nation, (4/25/16); "Beyond the Pilgrim Story, Text of the Mayflower Compact," Pilgrim Hall Museum, America's Museum of Pilgrim Possessions, http://www.pilgrimhallmuse-um.org/mayflower_compact_text.htm, (4/25/16).

who will stand for what's right but do it in kindness and love, instead of in ways that stir up more strife.

Then this country will once again be truly *one nation under God.*

TIME TO GROW UP

You might be thinking, *The Church—not just in America—but all over the world, has been squabbling for years. We'll never be in unity!*

According to Ephesians 4, there's coming a time (and it has to be soon because there's not much time left, now) when the Body of Christ *will* come together:

> …in the unity of the faith, and of the knowledge of the Son of God, unto a perfect [mature] man, unto the measure of the stature of the fulness of Christ: that we henceforth be no more children, tossed to and fro, and carried about with every wind of doctrine, by the sleight of men, and cunning craftiness, whereby they lie in wait to deceive; but speaking the truth in love,

may grow up into him in all things, which is the head, even Christ: from whom the whole body fitly joined together and compacted by that which every joint supplieth, according to the effectual working in the measure of every part, maketh increase of the body unto the edifying of itself in love (verses 13-16).

When the Church grows up into that kind of maturity, nothing will be able to stop us. We'll flood this earth with the glory of God. We'll preach the "gospel of the kingdom...in all the world for a witness unto all nations [or *ethnic groups*]; and then shall the end come" (Matthew 24:14). That's our destiny as His end-time Body on the earth—and according to Jesus, we're going to fulfill it.

To do so, however, we must be "fitly joined together," refusing to allow ourselves to be split into different camps and pitted against each other by the devil, who's attempting to deceive us into fighting with each other like a bunch of toddlers. If we allow ourselves to fall into his trap, we'll get stuck in a state of spiritual immaturity where we can't accomplish much for the kingdom of God. That's what happened to the Corinthian believers in the New Testament. The spirit of division so stunted their spiritual growth, the Apostle Paul wrote to them and said:

> I, brethren, could not speak unto you as unto spiritual,
> but as unto carnal, even as unto babes in Christ. I have
> fed you with milk, and not with meat: for hitherto ye
> were not able to bear it, neither yet now are ye able.
> For ye are yet carnal: for whereas there is among you
> envying, and strife, and divisions, are ye not carnal,
> and walk as men? For while one saith, I am of Paul;
> and another, I am of Apollos; are ye not carnal? (1
> Corinthians 3:1-4).

Talk about a sad state of affairs! Envying, strife and division
had reduced them to the place where, even though they were
born again and *had* grown in The LORD, they had begun
thinking like unbelievers again. As a result, Paul's ministry to them was hindered. He couldn't share with them the
life-changing revelations God had given him. The Corinthians had become too naturally minded. Paul knew their car-
nality would hinder them from comprehending the things
he wanted to teach them because the things of God must be
spiritually discerned (1 Corinthians 2:14).

What's more, the Corinthian believers didn't even realize they had a problem! They were actually proud of their sectarian splits and boasted, "I'm of this group" and "I'm of that group." They apparently thought that being either "of Paul" or "of Apollos" proved they were superior and uncompromising. In reality, they only proved they'd fallen prey to a spirit of judgment and segregation. They'd been *deceived by the spirit of division.*

Jesus said, "If a house be divided against itself, that house cannot stand" (Mark 3:25). That's the absolute, unchanging truth. A divided house *will* fall. It's not a probability, it's inevitable. And it's as true for believers today as it was for the Corinthians. If we operate in a spirit of division, our house becomes weak—and it *will* fall.

This became jarringly clear to me, personally, one day. I was praying and repenting before God about something critical I'd said about another believer. When I finished, God said to me, *It's a good thing you did that.* I could tell by the way He said it, He wanted me to know this is serious business. If I divided myself from someone else in His Body, I would guarantee my own failure—I would fall.

That's a dangerous thing to not know—and apparently, the Corinthians didn't know it. So Paul set them straight. In essence, he said to them, "I wanted to feed you spiritual meat from The WORD of God that would grow you up and make you strong, but you couldn't receive it. All I could do is give you a little spiritual milk because you'd let the spirit of division turn you into a bunch of babies! There was so much envying, strife and division among you, I couldn't do much for you."

Compare what Ephesians 4 says about "speaking the truth in love" to what Paul said there about "envying, and strife, and divisions." They're complete opposites. You can't do both at the same time. As you speak the truth in love, you grow up, or mature, spiritually. You move away from a spirit of division and into a spirit of love and reconciliation. By contrast, when you fight with other believers and separate yourself from them, you go the other direction. You move back into spiritual babyhood.

This is the goal of the devil's efforts to bring the spirit of division into the Church. That spirit works to divide and conquer by keeping believers acting like children, tossed to and fro by all kinds of doctrines and differences of opinion (Ephesians

4:14). It comes to infect us with its poison and get us into strife so we'll think and behave like mere unchanged men.

The devil has been doing a pretty good job of this for a long, long time, and lately he's stepped up his activities. But as 2 Corinthians 2:11 says, "We are not ignorant of his devices." We don't have to let him keep on tricking us with his divisive treachery. We can turn the situation around.

When our minds are renewed with the truth of God's WORD, we'll be better able to identify the devil's strategies. We'll be better equipped to drag the spirit of division out of the darkness, shine the light of God on it, and drive it out of our lives, our homes, our churches, and our communities. We can even exercise our God-given authority over what it's trying to do in our nation.

Jesus said, "All power [authority][3] is given unto me in heaven and in earth" (Matthew 28:18). As His disciples, we're joint heirs of that authority. So let's use it to thwart the devil's tactics and advance God's kingdom in these final, glorious days.

Let's put this snake in the grass to flight!

---

3 "power," Strong's, G1849; "power" *Vine's Expository Dictionary of Biblical Words* (Thomas Nelson: Nashville, 1985) No. 2 *exousia.*

CHAPTER 2

THE VARIETY IS WONDERFUL!

*Now ye are the body of Christ, and
members in particular.*

1 Corinthians 12:27

When it comes to waging military warfare, it's been wisely said that if you want to win, you must know your enemy. The same holds true for us as spiritual soldiers. The first thing we must do if we're going to deal effectively with the spirit of division is to learn how to recognize it. We have to be able to spot it in a split second every time it raises its ugly head.

You'll be glad to know, this isn't hard to do. It's easy, in fact, because the spirit of division—whether it's attacking a marriage, a church or a nation—always does the same thing: It magnifies differences between people in a spirit of discord and hate.

We already saw an example of this in the church at Corinth. The devil stirred up strife and division there by magnifying the differences between various preachers and ministries. Each minister appealed more to some people than to others because each had his own style and assignment from God. These ministers preached the same gospel, but they didn't all minister exactly the same thing in exactly the same way. As Paul explained it, "I have planted, Apollos watered; but God gave the increase" (1 Corinthians 3:6).

Since "planting" and "watering" ministries are different, the spirit of division exploited those differences. It magnified them in a hateful way to stir up trouble in the church. The people didn't realize what was happening, so they let that spirit con them. They divided up into denominational-like camps and started fighting with each other about which preacher was the best.

It was ironic, really. The spirit of division took what was designed by God to strengthen and unify that church and used it, instead, to weaken and divide it. The devil actually split that congregation by getting them to fight over differences divinely ordained to BLESS and bring them together. God *meant* for those ministers to be different from each other! Each of those preachers had a part, but together, their giftings could provide the church with a rich, well-rounded spiritual supply that would accelerate the church's spiritual growth.

That's always how it is in the Body of Christ. Not just ministers, but all believers, are members of a local body. We each have our own part, and when we do what God has anointed us to do, our differences fit together in a way that makes the body stronger. So when we work together, everyone gets BLESSED!

First Corinthians 12 puts it this way:

> Now there are diversities of gifts, but the same Spirit. And there are differences of administrations, but the same LORD. And there are diversities of operations, but it is the same God which worketh all in all. But the manifestation of the Spirit is given to every man to profit withal.... For as the body is one, and hath many members, and all the members of that one body, being many, are one body: so also is Christ (verses 4-7, 12).

The variety of gifts in the Body of Christ is wonderful! It's not surprising, though, because God has always created variety. You can see that by looking at how He made the human race. He wasn't content to create just one kind of man. Even though Adam, all by himself, reflected the totality of God's nature—both the masculine and feminine side—God said, "It is not good that the man should be alone" (Genesis 2:18). So, He put Adam into a deep sleep and took out one of his ribs. He separated the female part of Adam from the male part, and created a woman (or man with a womb). Then, He brought them together into relationship, where they were rejoined, and their union made them even better. Their differences put together, created greater strength.

Of course, recognizing the power in their unity, before long, the devil got involved. Sin entered the picture and messed things up. As a result, throughout the centuries, men and women have generally been divided. They've gotten into strife with each other and waged small wars over which gender is superior.

The truth is, both are superior.

In some ways women are superior to men. If you don't believe that, men, watch your wife have a baby. I've seen what that involves, and I wouldn't want to go through it for anything in the world! It would take a commitment to the perpetuating of the human race much stronger than my willingness to go through labor, delivery and all that involves! Every other man I know feels the same way. If it were up to the male of the species to bear children, the human race wouldn't last long at all. So, women are definitely superior.

Yet at the same time, men are superior, too. They're created to be and do things that women aren't. So both men and women have weaknesses, and both have strengths. Where the woman is strong, the man is weak. Where the man is strong, the woman is weak. When you put them together, there's no weakness. They are "heirs together of the grace of life" (1 Peter 3:7).

WHAT TEMPER IS TO STEEL

I can speak to this from personal experience. In the 50-plus years Gloria and I have been married, she has been strength to me. God told me she would be when He commissioned me into this ministry. Gloria has been to me what temper is to steel.

Before steel is tempered, it's brittle and worthless. It will break the first time any pressure is put on it. After it's tempered, however, it becomes just flexible enough so it won't break until it reaches its tensile strength. Like tempered steel, Gloria and I, together, are strong. We can do anything God asks us to do.

She's extremely practical and well-ordered, and I tend to be looser than a goose in a hailstorm. (It was a miracle she ever married me!) When I'm at home, for instance, I want everything spread out where I can see it. If you leave me in a room long enough, every drawer will be empty. I don't mind folding things up and keeping them neat, but I want things out on the table where I can see them.

Gloria is just the opposite. She likes everything put away and out of sight. So, after I take everything out, she comes in and puts it all away. I take it out. She puts it away. Together, we're strong in both the taking out and the putting away! If you need something taken out, you can call me. If you need it put away, you can call her. Between us, we can handle either one!

This is a humorous example, and we laugh about that sometimes, but in more significant areas of life, our differences have proven to be a vital spiritual advantage. Back in 1988, when The LORD told us to go on daily television, neither of us was ready for it. The very thought of being on TV—daily—made our heads spin. At that point in our ministry, I thought I already had enough to do, and I was certainly not looking for another assignment. Gloria knew how much it would cost and wasn't looking to spend that much money. So when God spoke to us, we each responded in our own way.

She immediately started figuring and planning what the budget would have to be. I didn't give those things a thought because that's not how I operate. I don't figure and plan. I just listen to The LORD and hang on to what He says. Eventually, something clicks inside me, and suddenly, I'm ready to go.

Gloria was still trying to work out the financial figures, when I sensed that inner click about the daily broadcasts. "Let's do it!" I said.

"We don't have the money," she replied.

"That doesn't matter. We have faith, don't we?"

"So, we're going to do this anyway?"

"Yeah, we are!" I said. She agreed, and we jumped into daily television together.

In the early days of our ministry, Gloria didn't always respond with a lot of enthusiasm to such conversations. She always obeyed God and took whatever leap of faith I was ready to make, but she did it saying, "Oh, dear Jesus...help us!" Now, she's up for any faith adventure—anytime, anywhere. When God speaks, she says, "Thank You, Jesus. Here we go!"

What caused her to change? For one thing, through the years, some of my "*it doesn't matter if we don't have any money, let's jump up and do it*" attitude has rubbed off on her. At the same time, a lot of her practicality has rubbed off on me. Now, we meet one another in the middle, where both of us are bold *and* practical.

That's what God had in mind for marriage all along. That's why His perfect plan for families includes a husband and wife, who are also father and mother, if they have children. He didn't plan for marriage to be a battleground. Husbands and wives are different, but their differences make the family stronger. The Bible doesn't say, "Children, obey your fathers," or "Children, obey your mothers." It says, "Children, obey your parents" (Ephesians 6:1). The father and mother have authority in the spirit realm—together.

It's no wonder the devil works so hard to invade Christian homes with the spirit of division! A husband and wife standing in unity on The WORD of God can build a home that can never be shaken. The two of them, in agreement, can bring anything to pass that's according to the will of God (Matthew 18:19).

TOGETHER, WE DON'T MISS A BEAT

These same basic truths apply to people of different races. Just as men and women have strengths that make them superior, all the various nationalities and racial ethnicities have strengths that make them superior. Each has been blessed by God to excel in certain ways. Yet, they're all different.

If we bring together a group of people of different races who have all witnessed the same event, each will interpret it differently. A person of one race might say, "This is what happened." But, a person of another race may say, "No, that's not the way it was at all." Another will say, "You're both wrong. I was there. I saw it, and *this* is what really happened."

The reason each group has such diverse perspectives is simple: They all come from different backgrounds and cultures. Their mindsets and thought patterns aren't the same. But, if the devil gets a chance, he'll magnify the differences in their perspectives and cause hate and discord among them. Pretty soon, the white folks, for example, who witnessed the event might be saying to each other, "Did you hear what that crazy Indian said? Isn't that the silliest thing you ever heard?" The black folks might be saying, "Did you hear what that white fool said? That's nuts!" The brown folks and yellow folks will be shaking their heads saying, "None of the rest of these guys know anything. This is the dumbest bunch of people I've ever met in my life." Eventually, the devil will have them all so divided against one another, it'll be impossible to bring them together to give the full story about what they saw.

However, if the Holy Spirit is allowed to work among them, He can turn the situation around. He can take the differences between those people and magnify them in love. Just as in the marriage scenario, He can get them into unity with each other and, together, they'll provide a more accurate picture of the event than any of the groups alone ever could.

I'm sometimes reminded of this when I'm in a worship service where black people and white people, for example, are singing and praising The LORD together. The white people tend to clap on the first and third beats, while the black people tend to clap on the second and fourth beats. Each group is clapping at different times—but together they don't miss a beat! (I learned that from Creflo Dollar.)

To me, that's a good picture of what can happen on every level when believers of different skin colors, nationalities or points of view *allow the Holy Spirit* to bring them into unity where they can learn from and share with one another. *Together*, they grow stronger and become more dangerous to the devil because they touch all bases, instead of just one here and there. *Together*, they're whole and complete with nothing missing. They become a force the devil can't reckon with.

It's time we realized this! For us to become truly powerful in the kingdom of God, and any great threat to the kingdom of darkness, we're going to have to grow up—together. It won't be enough for just a few of us to grow up on our own and say "too bad" about everyone else. It doesn't work that way. We're all part of each other. We're one body—the Body of Christ!

You may be wondering if I'm saying the Church needs to be less prejudiced and more racially integrated. "Prejudice" and "integration" are *secular words*. The world has been using them for years. Governments have bent over backward trying to deal with the problem they call "prejudice" by passing integration laws and *forcing* people to come together. Such laws are fine, as far as they go. But they've never really solved the problem. Despite the best efforts of governments and legislators, racial strife still continues breaking out. "We thought we fixed this!" they'll say. "So, why are people still fighting?"

They're still fighting because prejudice is not the root of the problem. Prejudice is the *result* of it. Prejudice is like the leaves on a tree. The root of the tree is the spirit of division, and integration, by itself, won't get rid of it. People can hate one another sitting side by side just the same as they can hate each other when they're on opposite sides of town. In the front of the bus or the back of the bus, hate is hate. You can allow a man to sit in the front of the bus, and the people behind him can still look him in the back of the head and hate every bone in his body. So, *until you deal with the spirit of division,* the problem will still be there.

NOT JUST INTEGRATION— RECONCILIATION!

To be clear, I'm not suggesting that integration laws aren't necessary. They're just not the ultimate solution. They can't be because they're not based on God's WORD. The word *integration* isn't found anywhere in the Bible. It doesn't say one thing to us about being integrated. It says we're to be *reconciled*—first to God, through faith in Jesus, and then to each other. That's what Redemption is all about.

According to the New Testament:

If any man be in Christ, he is a new creature: old things are passed away; behold, all things are become new. And all things are of God, who hath *reconciled* us to himself by Jesus Christ, and hath given to us the ministry of *reconciliation;* to wit, that God was in Christ, *reconciling* the world unto himself, not imputing their trespasses unto them; and hath committed unto us the word of *reconciliation.* Now then we are ambassadors for Christ, as though God did beseech you by us: we pray you in Christ's stead, be ye *reconciled* to God. For he hath made him to be sin for us, who knew no sin; that we might be made the righteousness of God in him (2 Corinthians 5:17-21).

Therefore if thou bring thy gift to the altar, and there rememberest that thy brother hath ought against thee; leave there thy gift before the altar, and go thy way; first be *reconciled* to thy brother, and then come and offer thy gift (Matthew 5:23-24).

When believers are reconciled in the Spirit and walking together in faith and love, the differences in our skin color and racial backgrounds are irrelevant because spiritually, we're one! We belong to the same spiritual family. We've been born of the seed of God's WORD. We share the same heavenly Father, and we've been made the righteousness of God in Christ Jesus. What we have in common in Christ is so powerful that our different cultural backgrounds don't amount to a hill of beans!

It doesn't matter the color of your skin or your racial background, as a born-again child of God, I don't have to be forced by an integration law to sit next to you. I sit next to you because God's love has been shed abroad in my heart, and I love you with His love. I truly want to know what God is saying to you and how you see things. This is particularly true if your natural heritage is different from mine because you *are* going to see things differently than I do, and I value your insight. I want to find out more about how you think so I can be a greater blessing to you, and together, we can be a greater blessing to the world.

This desire is what motivated me a number of years ago to learn more about how my ancestors thought. My grandfather was Cherokee, but I wasn't raised in that culture, so I didn't know much about it. The more I found out, the better I understood both my relatives and my own natural perspective. I realized, *That's the way I see things! I thought it was just me, but it's the influence of my Indian heritage!*

Best of all, learning to understand Indian thought patterns has helped me when I'm preaching to my Native American brothers and sisters in Christ. It's given me a clearer grasp of how they see things. As a result, we can communicate better and our different upbringings don't get in the way. One of my greatest joys for many years now, has been getting to preach with and work alongside great Native American ministers and believers. We've experienced some tremendous moves of God together.

Yet as much as I've come to love the Indian side of my family, I have the same kind of esteem for people in the Body of Christ whose bloodlines are so different from mine that the only blood we have in common is the blood of Jesus! I love and treasure them all—in all their wonderful variety.

Integration? That word doesn't even come close to describing the law of God that brings you and me together as members of God's multifaceted, multicolored spiritual family. We're brought together by the law of love. We're walking together in the Holy Spirit. Unlike the spirit of division, the Holy Spirit magnifies our differences in a way that draws us to one another in admiration and appreciation. No one has to force us to rub elbows with each other because *in Christ*—in the Anointed One and His Anointing—we've been reconciled. In every opportunity The LORD gives us, we want to be as close to one another as we can get!

CHAPTER 3

ABOVE ALL, GET WISDOM

For wisdom is a defence, and money is a defence: but the excellency of knowledge is, that wisdom giveth life to them that have it.

Ecclesiastes 7:12

If we could spend all our time with other believers, dealing with the spirit of division would be relatively simple. If the devil ever tried to get us to start fighting with each other, we could just continue to focus on our spiritual family ties. We could rejoice over the fact that, even though we may have our disagreements, everyone around us is born again and endeavoring to act (to some degree, anyway) like Jesus.

But, you know as well as I do, that's not the reality we're facing.

Christians don't live their whole lives inside the walls of a church. It's not what we're called to do. We've been commissioned to "go…into all the world, and preach the gospel to every creature" (Mark 16:15). We've been commanded by the Master Himself to get out there in the darkness, and let our light shine before men, that they may see our good works, and glorify our Father which is in heaven. Jesus said, we are the salt of the earth and the light of the world (Matthew 5:13-14).

It's an exciting assignment! But as we've all discovered, carrying it out in the midst of a world where the spirit of division is on the rampage can be rough. When ethnic groups are rising up against each other and ugly things are being said and done by people all around us, it's tempting to let ourselves be drawn into the conflict. This is especially true when some of the ugly things being said and done are purposely directed toward *us*. We can be tempted to react in the flesh and become part of the problem instead of the solution.

How do we make sure we don't fall prey to that temptation? How can we continue being the blessing Jesus called us to be when the very people we're trying to bless are yielding to the spirit of division and making *us* the targets of their racism, bigotry or hate?

Proverbs 4:7-9 gives us the answer:

> Wisdom is the principal thing; therefore get wisdom: and with all thy getting get understanding. Exalt her, and she shall promote thee: she shall bring thee to honour, when thou dost embrace her. She shall give to thine head an ornament of grace: a crown of glory shall she deliver to thee.

Notice, verse 7 says, "Wisdom is the principal thing." The word *principal* means "first, highest in rank, importance or value." It indicates when we have God's wisdom about a situation, we have the only thing that matters. When we have God's wisdom, we have something so powerful, no one and nothing in this world can keep us down.

This is the reason we, as believers, don't have to fight and get mad at people when the spirit of division uses them to try to oppress us in some way. We can keep walking in kindness and love because we have an advantage. As God's children, we have His supernatural wisdom available to us. We have His Holy Spirit inside us, and we have His written WORD. All we have to do is believe and do what God says, and His wisdom will protect and promote us.

We'll always come out on top of any situation if we obey God's commands and follow the promptings of the Holy Spirit. No matter how badly people may treat us or how high the odds seem to be stacked against us, if we'll operate according to the wisdom of God, we'll be BLESSED. The Bible confirms this in scripture after scripture:

- "And it shall come to pass, if thou shalt hearken diligently unto the voice of The LORD thy God, to observe and to do all his commandments which I command thee this day, that The LORD thy God will set thee on high above all nations of the earth: And all these blessings shall come on thee, and overtake thee, if thou shalt hearken unto the voice of The LORD thy God....The LORD shall make thee the head, and not the tail; and thou shalt be above only, and thou shalt not be beneath; if that thou hearken unto the commandments of The LORD thy God..." (Deuteronomy 28:1-2, 13).

- "[The WORD of God] shall not depart out of thy mouth; but thou shalt meditate therein day and night, that thou mayest observe to do according to all that is written therein: for then thou shalt make thy way prosperous, and then thou shalt have good success" (Joshua 1:8).

- "No weapon that is formed against thee shall prosper; and every tongue that shall rise against thee in judgment thou shalt condemn. This is the heritage of the servants of The LORD, and their righteousness is of me, saith The LORD" (Isaiah 54:17).

- "For this is the love of God, that we keep his commandments: and his commandments are not grievous. For whatsoever is born of God overcometh the world: and this is the victory that overcometh the world, even our faith" (1 John 5:3-4).

You might be thinking, *Yeah, I know the Bible says those things, but right now it seems like everyone is against me. They're prejudiced against my skin color. They discriminate against me because I grew up on the wrong side of the tracks. No one will even give me a job. I've gotten to the point where I'm hopeless!*

No, you're not hopeless!

No one is hopeless because they're in a bad situation. No one is hopeless because they're being discriminated against, or because they don't have a job. Hopelessness doesn't come from those kinds of things. Hopelessness, in the truest sense of the word, comes from being outside the kingdom of God. It comes from being in the condition all of us were in before we were born again. As Ephesians 2:12 says, "At that time ye were without Christ, being aliens from the commonwealth of Israel, and strangers from the covenants of promise, having no hope, and without God in the world."

Talk about a reason to be hopeless! That's it, right there.

People who are "without Christ...and without God in the world" are trapped in a world full of trouble. Because they're outside the New Covenant, they're dependent on a Babylonian world system in which people try to meet their own needs without God. They're being lorded over by the devil, who is the "god of this world" (2 Corinthians 4:4). And, he's a ruthless tyrant. He makes people fight and scratch for everything they get—and once they get it, he steals it from them.

When you're in that situation and you lose your job, or the economy falls apart, or you encounter some kind of mistreatment or racism, it *is* a bad deal. You don't have any way out. You don't have a covenant with God to depend on, and you can't see any way to triumph over the forces that are coming against you.

But it's a whole different story once you receive Jesus as your Savior and LORD. In Him "are hid all the treasures of wisdom and knowledge" (Colossians 2:3). So when you're in union with Him and you're hearing His voice, He can tell you how to overcome anything the devil and the world's system can throw at you. God can show you the secret to walking in triumph through *every* situation.

GETTING PROMOTED
AND SAVING LIVES

I'm thinking right now about a man I know whose life illustrated walking in triumph through difficult situations in a marvelous way. He was a three-star general in the U.S. Army. As a black man growing up in the southern part of the United States before the civil rights movement, he faced challenges most people would consider insurmountable. I met him some 30-plus years ago, just after he retired, and I was thrilled over the opportunity to sit down and visit with him. Eager to know his story, I asked him about it.

He told me he'd been born into a Bible-believing Pentecostal family. His parents loved him and raised him well, but they didn't have the money to send him to college. So with barely enough formal education to qualify, he enlisted in the U.S. Army at a very young age.

He started out as a buck private but soon began moving up the ranks. From private, he was promoted to private first class. Then, he was promoted to corporal, then to staff sergeant and master sergeant. After that, he got a commission and began to advance further. "How did you manage to do it?" I asked.

"How did you go from being an enlisted man without any college degrees to where you are today?"

"I did it by laying hold of the wisdom of God by praying in the Holy Spirit," he said.

He illustrated what he meant by sharing a story with me I'll never forget. It centered around an experience he had during the Vietnam War. He had been an artillery captain, and one day, an infantry patrol in his area was surrounded by the Viet Cong. The young man leading the patrol had called in on the radio: "Captain, I don't know how we're going to get out of here," he said. "Our only hope is for you to lay an artillery barrage and open up an escape route for us. But if you tell me over the radio what direction I'm supposed to go, the VC will hear it. They'll meet us there and wipe us out. We don't have a chance."

I had been in the military myself, and as the general described this situation, I was on the edge of my seat. "What did you do?" I asked him.

"I told the patrol leader to hang on for a minute and promised to get right back to him," he said. "Then, I walked outside and got by myself so I could think and pray. I knew I had more firepower than anyone in the area and could totally annihilate the enemy threat if I used it. But in the process, I'd kill the men in our own patrol. Looking up into the night sky at the brilliance of the stars, I said, 'Jesus, I have a problem here. What's the solution?'

"For the next few minutes I walked back and forth under the stars, praying in tongues and speaking God's WORD. Suddenly, I saw the answer. I ran back inside and got on the radio. 'Lieutenant, are you a Christian?' I asked.

"Yes, sir!"

"Do you know where our star arose in Bethlehem?"

"Yes, sir!"

"I'm going to lay an artillery barrage in every point of the compass but that one. You understand me, Lieutenant?"

"Affirmative, sir! I'm on my way!"

The plan worked perfectly. He released an artillery barrage to the north, south and west, and left a hole open to the east. The infantry patrol walked out in that direction, safe and sound! The VC couldn't do anything about it because they didn't know where the barrage was going to be. They had to take cover until the shells quit falling.

That's the wisdom of God—and it turned a buck private into a three-star general! It empowered that man to be BLESSED and to be a blessing to the people around him, despite all the obstacles the devil threw into his path.

After he finished telling me his story, I asked, "Did they ever give you any trouble because of your skin color or because you were Pentecostal?"

"They did when I was young," he said. "But they didn't give me any flack after I became a major, and then a lieutenant colonel, and then a general. They may still have been saying things about me, but I didn't hear any of it."

HERE TO SHOW THEM THE WAY OUT

Through the years, as I've thought about the general's story, a particular thing has stood out to me about it. The night he was praying out under the stars in Vietnam, he didn't get God's wisdom because he had himself on his mind. He didn't get it because he was wringing his hands and saying, "Oh God, what am I going to do? This whole patrol is going to get killed, and they're going to blame it on me. They're going to demote me back to private."

No, the general was attending to more important issues. He had a job to do and a calling to fulfill. He had people looking to him for help. He wasn't fretting over what someone might be thinking about him. He was totally focused on saving lives in the midst of a difficult situation.

The same should be true of every believer. Although we may not be in a Vietnamese jungle, rescuing soldiers in danger of being mowed down by enemy fire, spiritually we're in a similar situation. All around us, people are under assault by the devil. Those who aren't born again don't have any defense against him. They're trapped in his ungodly world system.

As citizens of heaven, we're here to show them the way out! That's the only reason we're still on this planet—to share the good news with people. We are to let them know, not only with our words, but with our lives that, through Jesus, we can all be reconciled to God *and to each other*. That's a revelation that multiplied millions of people don't have. They don't realize they can have a covenant with God. They don't know that by giving their lives to Jesus and walking in His wisdom, they can live a truly abundant life.

Jesus said, "If ye continue in my WORD, then are ye my disciples indeed; and ye shall know the truth, and the truth shall make you free" (John 8:31-32). But most people are looking for freedom in all the wrong places. They think it's what other people are doing to them and saying about them that's holding them captive. They think they're being held back by other people's attitudes toward them, or by their financial status, gender, lack of education, or ethnicity.

Can society's prejudices about those areas of our lives cause difficulties? Certainly they can. Racism can especially cause difficulties—whether it's based on skin color, economic class, or anything else. It can create tremendous difficulty. Its effects can be extremely painful and hard to overcome. But, if we lay hold of the wisdom of God, it can empower us to *rise above* the hardness.

I'm thinking right now about another man who, like the

three-star general I met, demonstrated this throughout his life. His name is Johnny Johnson, a former United States assistant secretary of the Navy (Manpower and Reserve Affairs). Some years ago, he wrote a book entitled *Beyond Defeat*.[4] If you've never read it, you need to. It's the kind of book that, along with the Bible, should be required reading for every born-again child of God.

In the book, Johnny tells about his dad, a very tall, powerful man of God, whose ancestry was African Watusi. He was in his 60s by the time Johnny was born and had gained a lot of godly wisdom. That wisdom proved especially valuable in the early years of Johnny's life when he ran into trouble in school.

The family had moved into a small, but really tough community in the southern part of the United States. Johnny had never been in that situation before, and when the little white boys in the school started giving him a hard time, he didn't know what to do.

As I remember the story, he went to his dad for help. "Daddy, they call me terrible names!" he said.

4 *Beyond Defeat,* James E. Johnson (Nampa: Pacific Press Publishing Association, 2001).

"Well, son, they can't help that."

"They can't? Why not?" Johnny had asked.

"Because of their light skin," his dad had explained. "It doesn't protect them from the sun, so in this hot climate, their brains overheat in the middle of the day. They can't really do anything about it, but you can help them. When those little fellows' brains start heating up, pray for them and be kind to them."

Johnny took his father's counsel to heart. From then on, when the boys at school said ugly things to him, he refused to let it bother him. He'd just think, *Wow, their heads must be about to pop! That must be why they're so mad!* Then he'd just love them and say, "Can I help you? Can I get you some water or something?"

Over time, the white kids started to like him. By the end of the year, he was the hero of the school. Of course, he eventually figured out the white kids' brains weren't really overheating, but by then, he'd learned that love truly is beyond defeat.

After he graduated, Johnny Johnson joined the Unites States Marine Corps. He not only went through the hellishness of combat, he did it when segregation was still a fact of life in the military. Actually, Johnny was one of the reasons the color barrier was broken down in the Marine Corps. He won more Marines to Jesus than anyone else on record.

He became assistant secretary of the Navy under President Richard Nixon's administration, at a strategic time in our nation. Racial tension was escalating aboard some of the U.S. warships in the 7th Fleet, and no one knew what to do about it.[5]

Johnny and his personnel director decided it was time to update their files on the fleet's status, needs, activities and problems, and develop relationships with the command staff so they would feel comfortable discussing some of these issues with him. An inspection team would visit the fleet's bases to gather information and discuss solutions.

The 7th Fleet was headquartered in Honolulu, and its area covered Guam, Okinawa, Japan, Korea, Hong Kong and other areas in the Pacific that housed American bases. Johnny and his inspection team flew into Honolulu, where he met with the admiral who briefed Johnny on the problems he

---

5 *Black Sailor, White Navy: Racial Unrest in the Fleet During the Vietnam War Era,* John Sherwood (New York: NYU Press, 2007).

was having and what he needed help with—including racial challenges among the personnel. Johnny was scheduled to inspect the fleet, and learned that he was the first black man to ever inspect a U.S. naval fleet.

From Honolulu, the inspection team flew on to Guam to meet with the resident admiral. According to military protocol, the top ranking officer on the plane disembarks first, so Johnny got off the plane and walked down the ramp. The admiral, who was standing there waiting for the secretary along with his top commanders and officers, looked right past him. The two had never met, and the admiral, seeing a black man, assumed he couldn't possibly be Secretary Johnson, and continued looking for him among the disembarking passengers.

Johnny realized what was going on, but rather than embarrass the man, walked just past him and stood waiting while everyone else got off the plane. When it became clear no one else was left on board, the admiral looked around nervously, as if trying to figure out what to do. He finally asked Johnny's senior aide, "Are you the secretary?" Johnny's aide answered, "No, sir, that's the secretary standing over there," pointing to Johnny. The admiral hesitated, and then seeing that Secretary Johnson was not initiating introduction, the admiral, far outranked, began walking toward Johnny, apologizing that he hadn't been told Johnny was black. At Johnny's prompting, the admiral hesitantly admitted he had thought Johnny was a steward who had come along to help serve.[6]

As his superior officer, Johnny could have lectured the admiral up one side and down the other for not recognizing him when he got off the airplane. Nine out of 10 men would have. But Johnny was listening to the Spirit of God.

Johnny told me that in spite of his graciousness, however, the admiral held on to his bigotry. Johnny didn't respond. He got off by himself in his room and prayed in the spirit. He just lay there on his bunk and thought about the admiral and started surrounding him with the love of God. Johnny covered him up in his prayer time with the love of God.

At dinner that night, after the meal was over and he'd visited with everyone else, Johnny stopped by the admiral's table. Leaning close, he spoke to the admiral quietly so that no one else could hear: "I know you have a lot of trouble to deal with right now, and I'm not here to add to it. I'm not here to hurt you. I'm here to help you." The admiral came over and sat

---

6 *Beyond Defeat*, p. 206.

down next to him, with tears running down his cheeks. He said, "My God, Mr. Johnson, can you ever forgive me?"

God's love works in the toughest situations. Johnny told me about a particularly difficult situation he dealt with during that season of his career that he encountered on the *USS Forrestal*. Racial tensions on that particular ship had erupted into violence. One young sailor had been critically injured when he was hit with a pipe, and his skull was fractured. When Johnny arrived, the man was lying in the dispensary, near death. No one had yet figured out who hit him.

With the whole place teetering on the edge of a race war, Johnny called everyone together on the fantail of the ship. Then, he began reading to the 1200 men standing in front of him from the New Testament about the love of God. For a while, the more Johnny talked about God's love, the harder the men's faces became. As he said, when he told me the story, "I didn't know if they were going to throw me overboard, or what."

Realizing he needed additional wisdom from God, he backed off for a few minutes and prayed in the Holy Ghost. Then, he addressed the men again. "Jesus died for you because He loves you," he told them. "But I want you to know that because of

Him, I love you, too. I'd have died for you when I was in the Marine Corps, and I'd die for you today."

With those words, the power of God hit, and men began to fall on their faces. Johnny gave an invitation, and sailors started getting born again and baptized in the Holy Spirit. Then, they started getting healed. Before long, black sailors and white sailors were throwing their arms around each other and dancing in the spirit together.

Suddenly, one of them jumped up and screamed: "Oh, Secretary Johnson, come help me! Hurry! Hurry!"

"What's wrong?" asked Johnny.

"A few days ago, I almost killed that white boy! He's down there in the dispensary now with his head busted open! We need to go pray for him!"

They ran down to the dispensary, and a whole group of them gathered around the injured man's bunk, caught hands and prayed. God miraculously healed the man, and he completely recovered. They went out and spread the news all over the 7th Fleet about the *USS Forrestal* revival!

There had been problems of some kind in every area Johnny and his team had visited. But, on every ship, they had initiated a prayer breakfast and had a great time.

Why did all that happen?

It happened because Johnny Johnson's dad pressed in to The WORD of God and prayed in the Holy Spirit! He got the wisdom of God about how to raise a child in the middle of a culture of bigotry where people were being dominated by the spirit of division. He planted God's wisdom in his son's heart and taught him that love is beyond defeat.

In the back of Johnny's book, you'll find page after page listing his accomplishments. You'll read how he became "The first black man…" to do this, and "The first black man…" to do that. Having broken all kinds of racial barriers, Johnny has been a blessing to countless numbers of people. Receiving more than 800 awards in the past 25 years for outstanding achievement and significant service to his country, Johnny has overcome the spirit of division, brought people together and demonstrated, time and again, what the wisdom of God can do.

What a man! What a life! What a testimony!

EXAMPLES WORTH FOLLOWING

Well," someone might say, "it's nice to hear about people like Johnny Johnson and the three-star general you met, but those are isolated instances."

No, they're not. I could tell you about any number of other people who've risen above the ugliness of racism in much the same way those men did. During World War II, for example, there was a whole group of them in the United States Army Air Forces. They were called the Tuskegee Airmen.[7] The Air Forces initially brought them together as an experiment to see if black men could learn how to pilot airplanes.

Obviously, the very basis of the experiment was racist and insulting (not to mention, stupid!). But rather than take offense, the Tuskegee Airmen made up their minds to become the best pilots the United States Army Air Forces had ever seen. Under the command of Benjamin O. Davis Jr.,[8] who later became the first black general in the U.S. Air Force, they worked so hard and became so good at what they did, the Air Force soon sent them to Europe.

---

7 "Who Were They?" The Tuskegee Airmen National Historical Museum, http://www.tuskegeemuseum.org/who-were-they/, (5/4/16).
8 *Benjamin O. Davis Jr.: Air Force General and Tuskegee Airmen Leader (Military Heroes),* Sari Earl (Edina: Abdo Publishing Co., 2010).

They served in the 352nd Special Operations Wing as air cover for B-17s on bombing runs to Germany. From their first daylight precision bombing mission, they never lost a bomber. This was phenomenal. Previously, bombers were being lost at a rate of 50 to 60 percent.

One of the first pilots the Tuskegee group flew cover for didn't know who they were, but he realized right away they were good. He was coming back from Germany to England after one of the engines on his plane had been shot out and some enemy planes came after him. A couple of the Tuskegee pilots saw what was happening, shot down the enemy planes, and got him back home safely.

When they landed, the pilot who'd had the damaged engine went to thank the pilots who'd helped him. There was no mistaking the planes they were flying because the tails were painted red. When he got to the planes, however, he was confused because all he found were two black men. This was 1941, and as a white pilot, he'd never seen a black pilot before.

One of them said to him, "Were you in that B-17 that almost went down over there?"

"Yeah," he answered.

"Well, I'm the one who helped you."

Looking even more confused, the white pilot said, "No. I want to see the pilot who was flying the plane." Eventually, he just walked away dumbfounded. *Black pilots?* He didn't know what to think about that.

A while later, that same white pilot was assigned to fly the first bombing mission over Berlin. When he realized the 352nd wing wasn't scheduled to fly cover for him, he went to the colonel in charge of the mission and objected. "Excuse me, sir," he said, "but I have nine other men aboard this airplane that I'm responsible for. If I'm going to Berlin, I want the Tuskegee Airmen on my cover, so I am respectfully requesting the 352nd accompany us."

The colonel agreed, and Benjamin O. Davis flew the mission. Right on the nose of his airplane, painted in big letters, were the words "By Request." Sure enough, they flew to Berlin and back without losing a man.

Do you think the wisdom of God had something to do with all that? Certainly, it did! If you doubt that, ask Daniel "Chappie" James, Jr.[9] He was the first four-star black general

9 "Daniel "Chappie" James, Jr." The National Aviation Hall of Fame: Honoring Aerospace Legends to Inspire Future Leaders, http://www.nationalaviation.org/james-jr-daniel/ (5/5/16).

in the United States Armed Forces. He's one of only a handful of generals ever, whose rank was high enough to give orders to the president of the United States.

One person Chappie credited for his success was his little Holy Ghost-filled mother. When he was growing up in Florida, she'd invite the neighborhood kids who didn't have any place to go to school, to gather in her backyard. She'd teach them how to read and write, and tell them, "You're somebody! You're somebody in God! Whenever He gives you an opportunity to do something, you take it and give it everything you've got. Work at it with all your heart."

Three generals came out of that backyard!

One of them came into Chappie's office one day. He'd just received his third star and Chappie had just gotten his fourth. As they were congratulating each other, they both agreed if it hadn't been for Mama James, they would never have gotten those stars. She was the one who taught them that it didn't matter where they started out in life, if they'd seek God and keep walking with Jesus, He'd promote them.

Actually, what Mama James taught those generals was much

like what the Apostle Paul wrote in 1 Corinthians 1:24-25: "Christ [the Anointed One and His Anointing is] the power of God, and the wisdom of God," and "the foolishness of God is wiser than men."

> For ye see your calling, brethren, how that not many wise men after the flesh, not many mighty, not many noble, are called: But God hath chosen the foolish things of the world to confound the wise; and God hath chosen the weak things of the world to confound the things which are mighty; and base things of the world, and things which are despised, hath God chosen, yea, and things which are not, to bring to nought things that are: that no flesh should glory in his presence. But of him are ye in Christ Jesus, who of God is made unto us wisdom, and righteousness, and sanctification, and redemption: that, according as it is written, He that glorieth, let him glory in The LORD (verses 26-31).

Every time I think of believers like Chappie James, Johnny Johnson and others like them, I'm inspired by their examples. They not only overcame the spirit of division and walked in

God's BLESSING in their own lives, they became a blessing to countless others. When bigotry and racism tried to keep them down, they rose above it. They became salt in the earth and light in dark places—by the wisdom and the Anointing of God!

CHAPTER 4

A LESSON FROM THE MASTER

But whoso hath this world's good, and seeth his brother have need, and shutteth up his bowels of compassion from him, how dwelleth the love of God in him? My little children, let us not love in word, neither in tongue; but in deed and in truth.

1 John 3:17-18

W e've all felt the sting that comes from being targeted by the spirit of division. But of course, we haven't all felt it to the same degree. Some have had it easier than others.

In my life, for instance, my skin color has never really been an issue. Although I have Cherokee blood, about the only time I felt disrespected was as a youngster when I went to the movies. It bothered me that in the Westerns, when the Indians defeated the cowboys it was called a "massacre," and when the cowboys defeated the Indians it was called a "victory." But otherwise, my ethnicity never caused me any real problems. But now, I go into some parts of the United States where I know how they feel about Indian folks, and I start getting this creepy feeling—and I'd rather get on out of there. But I have to stop myself from thinking that way. That's thinking like a poor man. We need to learn to think like God because we've been made the righteousness of God (2 Corinthians 5:21).

When it comes to spiritual matters, however, it's another story. As a preacher, I've had to deal with religious racism, or prejudice, a lot. Over the years, I've been shunned by whole denominations and told I wasn't welcome in their churches. I've been called names, ridiculed and lied about, both verbally and in print. My ministry has even been harassed by a member of the United States Senate.

Yet, I want to be clear: While none of those things have been pleasant, they don't even compare to what many believers have experienced. There are Christians all over this planet who've faced so much bigotry and persecution that they might say to me, "You talk about rising above racism, but you don't know how I feel. You don't understand how badly I've been treated and what I've been through."

Do you know how I'd answer those dear people? I'd tell them they're absolutely right. Just based on my own experience, I don't know what they've been through. But, Jesus does. What He faced as our Savior, Redeemer and High Priest was worse than anything *any* human being will *ever* suffer. He "endured from sinners such grievous opposition and bitter hostility" it cost every last drop of His blood (Hebrews 12:3, *The Amplified Bible, Classic Edition*).

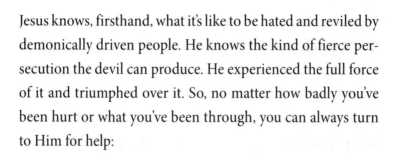

Jesus knows, firsthand, what it's like to be hated and reviled by demonically driven people. He knows the kind of fierce persecution the devil can produce. He experienced the full force of it and triumphed over it. So, no matter how badly you've been hurt or what you've been through, you can always turn to Him for help:

> Because He Himself [in His humanity] has suffered in being tempted (tested and tried), He is able [immediately] to run to the cry of (assist, relieve) those who are being tempted and tested and tried [and who therefore are being exposed to suffering].... For we do not have a High Priest Who is unable to understand and sympathize and have a shared feeling with our weaknesses and infirmities and liability to the assaults of temptation, but One Who has been tempted in every respect as we are, yet without sinning (Hebrews 2:18; 4:15, *The Amplified Bible, Classic Edition*).

Jesus is the Master! He not only conquered sin, He totally defeated satan. He crushed underfoot the spirit of division that's behind racism, and He can teach every one of us how to keep it under our feet, too.

People might wonder how Jesus can teach us about racism if that word isn't even in the Bible. Well, let's look at Luke 10:25. It records a conversation Jesus had where He addressed the issue of racism head-on without even mentioning the word. The conversation began one day when Jesus was ministering when "a certain lawyer stood up, and tempted him, saying, Master, what shall I do to inherit [be an heir of] eternal life?"

The word *tempted* in that verse indicates the lawyer's question wasn't really sincere. He obviously wasn't actually looking for an answer. He was trying to back Jesus into a doctrinal corner by asking Him an illogical question. "What should I *do* to inherit...?"

Every lawyer, and especially these experts in Jewish law at the time, knows that from a legal perspective such a question makes no sense. No one becomes an heir because of what they do. People become heirs because of who they are. In the natural, for example, I'm A.W. Copeland's heir. I inherited my portion of his estate, not because I did something, but simply because I'm his son and he's my dad. I was born of him.

Spiritually, I'm an heir of God for the same reason. I didn't earn the right to be God's child. I didn't qualify to inherit His

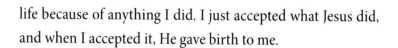

life because of anything I did. I just accepted what Jesus did, and when I accepted it, He gave birth to me.

Being born again is the only way to inherit eternal life. Yet, as we're about to see, Jesus didn't mention this to the lawyer. He didn't say, as He did to Nicodemus, "Ye must be born again" (John 3:7), because the lawyer wasn't really seeking God. He was just looking for a legalistic, religious debate. So, instead of talking to him about the new birth, Jesus accommodated him:

> He said unto him, What is written in the law? how readest thou? And he answering said, Thou shalt love The LORD thy God with all thy heart, and with all thy soul, and with all thy strength, and with all thy mind; and thy neighbour as thyself. And he said unto him, Thou hast answered right: this do, and thou shalt live (Luke 10: 26-28).

Jesus might have ended the conversation with those words, but the lawyer wasn't satisfied. He knew Jesus had a reputation for being kind to people who didn't deserve it and loving people considered by most religious Jews of that day to be no better than dogs. So in order to justify himself, the lawyer said to Jesus, "Who is my neighbour?"

And Jesus answering said, A certain man went down from Jerusalem to Jericho, and fell among thieves, which stripped him of his raiment, and wounded him, and departed, leaving him half dead. And by chance there came down a certain priest that way: and when he saw him, he passed by on the other side. And likewise a Levite, when he was at the place, came and looked on him, and passed by on the other side. But a certain Samaritan, as he journeyed, came where he was: and when he saw him, he had compassion on him, and went to him, and bound up his wounds, pouring in oil and wine, and set him on his own beast, and brought him to an inn, and took care of him. And on the morrow when he departed, he took out two pence, and gave them to the host, and said unto him, Take care of him; and whatsoever thou spendest more, when I come again, I will repay thee. Which now of these three, thinkest thou, was neighbour unto him that fell among the thieves? And [the lawyer] said, He that showed mercy on him. Then said Jesus unto him, Go, and do thou likewise (verses 30-37).

GOING THE SECOND MILE

You might be thinking, *I don't really see what all that has to do with racism.*

It has everything to do with it! Racism was rampant between Jews and Samaritans in Jesus' day. The Jews viewed the Samaritans as half-breeds who were both racially and religiously inferior. The Samaritans, in turn, hated the Jews. The two groups detested each other so much they lived in separate parts of the country and practiced a segregated lifestyle.

The Jewish lawyer was caught up in this mess. When it came to Samaritans, he was a bigot to the bone. Yet he prided himself on keeping the Ten Commandments. He probably thought since no Samaritans lived in *his* neighborhood, he could totally despise them and still legally claim he loved his neighbors.

Jesus confronted this ungodly perspective by telling him about the Good Samaritan. I strongly suspect the lawyer may have actually known the man. Maybe he had even been involved in the incident some way!

Whatever the case may have been, one thing is for sure: Had the situation been reversed and a Samaritan ambushed and wounded by thieves, the lawyer would not have come to the rescue. What's more, he knew it…which left him in a bind. How could he, as a self-respecting Jew, consider Samaritans to be his neighbors? He couldn't go around showing compassion to Samaritans! That was unthinkable. It wasn't in his nature. He was too bigoted.

This, of course, was the root of the lawyer's problem. He needed a new nature. He needed to believe in Jesus and be born again. Then, he'd be able to love his neighbors (Samaritans included) as himself.

One of the many great advantages of being a born-again believer is that because Love Himself lives in us, we can love anyone, anywhere, at any time. We can love everyone from the beggar on the street corner to the braggart in the corner office. After all, "the love of God is shed abroad in our hearts by the Holy Ghost" (Romans 5:5). We've inherited our heavenly Father's nature. We're love children of a love God, and we have inside us everything it takes to keep *all* His commandments.

Many Christians feel that the word *commandment* just sounds too hard and complicated, and believe the Ten Commandments are not applicable to us under the new covenant.

Certainly, we're under the new covenant. But that doesn't mean we should just forget about God's commandments. On the contrary, in the New Testament, we're repeatedly reminded of them. In John 14:21, for example, Jesus said to His disciples just before He went to the cross, "He that hath my commandments, and keepeth them, he it is that loveth me." And, 1 John 3:23 says, "This is his commandment, That we should believe on the name of his Son Jesus Christ, and love one another, as he gave us commandment."

Romans 13 adds:

> For this, Thou shalt not commit adultery, Thou shalt not kill, Thou shalt not steal, Thou shalt not bear false witness, Thou shalt not covet; and if there be any other commandment, it is briefly comprehended in this saying, namely, Thou shalt love thy neighbour as thyself. Love worketh no ill to his neighbour: therefore love is the fulfilling of the law (verses 9-10).

Somehow, the Ten Commandments have gotten a bad reputation in recent years. Because of how they've been presented, people have gotten the impression God uses them to bully us. They think He holds them over us like a big stick, with the attitude that, "If you make just one wrong move and break even one of My commandments, you're in big trouble!"

But that's contrary to the nature of God. It's not an accurate picture of our covenant relationship with Him. Our covenant with Him is based on His overwhelming desire to BLESS us! It's designed to lift us up, not beat us down.

If you want to see a picture of our covenant with God, look at the covenant He made with Abraham. Under that covenant, not only did Abraham commit everything he had to God, God committed everything He had to Abraham. Although Abraham obviously got the better end of the deal, that's what God wanted. His sole purpose in instigating the covenant was to BLESS Abraham and, ultimately, all mankind—including you and me.

Galatians 3 explains it:

> Now to Abraham and his seed were the promises

made. He saith not, And to seeds, as of many; but as of one, And to thy seed, which is Christ.... And if ye be Christ's, then are ye Abraham's seed, and heirs according to the promise (verses 16, 29).

Once we realize what it actually means to be an "heir according to the promise," keeping God's commandments ceases to be hard and complicated. We stop worrying about how much it's going to cost us to love our neighbor and begin thinking, *What does it matter how much it costs? I'm limitless! I'm in covenant with God. He'll supply me with everything I need to love people and be a blessing to them. Then, He'll bless me in return for doing it!*

This is what Paul was trying to get across in Ephesians 6:8 where he said, "Whatsoever good thing any man doeth, the same shall he receive of The LORD." That's what Jesus was talking about when He said, "If any man will sue thee at the law, and take away thy coat, let him have thy cloak also. And whosoever shall compel thee to go a mile, go with him twain" (Matthew 5:40-41).

Jesus is telling us in those verses to change our thinking, to mentally get rid of the shortage. He is telling us to get rid of the idea that if we only have two coats and we give both of them away, we'll end up freezing all winter. Get a revelation of the fact that if you give both coats in Jesus' Name, you'll end up with more coats than you can use because the supply that comes back to you for giving the second coat will be even greater than it was for giving the first one.

The same will be true about the miles. The reward for going the second mile with someone will be even bigger than it was for going the first mile. Why? Because when you break out of the legalistic, miserly mentality of doing as little for others as you can and start looking for more opportunities to love people and give to them, you're walking in faith and in the love of God. You're walking in His covenant of BLESSING. You're seeing what He really had in mind when He gave the Ten Commandments.

God wasn't saying, "Don't you dare steal. Don't you dare covet. If you do, I'll kill you!" He wasn't issuing threats. He was talking to people who were in covenant with Him, and basically saying:

> *I'm your Provider. I'm your Protector. So, stay in this with Me, and we'll do this together. Don't violate My loving nature by doing harm to other people. Don't*

get outside this covenant where I can't help you. You don't have to covet that other fellow's wife. I'll get you one even better looking than she is. You don't have to steal. I'll give you every good thing your heart desires. If someone steals from you, forgive them, consider what they stole to be a gift, and I'll replenish it a hundredfold. I love you with everything I have. So love Me with everything you have. Love your neighbor, and let Me love your neighbor through you. I'll supply you to supply him!

IT DOESN'T START WITH YOUR FEELINGS

The Good Samaritan had somehow caught hold of this revelation. He understood the value of going the second mile. So, he went beyond just doing his civic duty by telling the authorities about the man he saw lying injured at the side of the road. He tended to the man himself. He "had compassion on him" (Luke 10:33).

What exactly does it mean to *have compassion?*

First, let me tell you what it doesn't mean. It doesn't mean to be overcome with warm feelings about someone. Although emotions may eventually be involved, that's not where compassion starts. It starts when we make a decision to rise above our feelings. It begins when we decide we're going to act on the love of God within us, regardless of our current emotional state. It's acting in God's love—not out of negative emotions—even in the face of racism and strife.

If you want to see a picture of compassion, read about what Jesus did after He received the news that His cousin, John, had been brutally murdered by Herod and "he departed thence by ship into a desert place apart" (Matthew 14:13). Yet, "when the people had heard thereof, they followed him on foot out of the cities. And Jesus went forth, and saw a great multitude, and was moved with *compassion* toward them, and he healed their sick" (verses 13-14).

Jesus was not any less human than we are. He experienced the same emotions we would have in those circumstances. That's why He got into a boat and left town. He wanted to be alone and pray. But He'd made a decision to do, in every situation, what His Father did. So when sick people showed up, He acted on that decision and healed them.

Compassion is not a feeling, it's a person. God is love.

If we're going to live by the law of compassion, God's own love in us, we'll have to do the same. We'll have to make the decision to be moved by compassion, and nothing else, because many times our emotions will go 100 percent in the opposite direction.

Think how the Samaritan must have felt when he first spotted the man lying in the ditch. He didn't know who the man was. Because the thieves had stripped him of his clothing, the man didn't have anything on him that might indicate his social status. So, the Samaritan didn't know whether the man was rich or poor, good or bad. He didn't know whether he was a gentile, another Samaritan or a Jewish racist who'd just as soon spit on him as look at him.

But it didn't matter. He made a decision to *love his neighbor*. And because of that decision, he went over to help the man.

This is what compassion does—it goes! It takes action.

For the Samaritan, taking action meant putting a bleeding stranger on his own donkey. (Today's equivalent would be putting him into your car.) It meant bandaging the fellow's

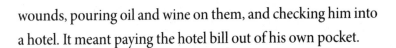

wounds, pouring oil and wine on them, and checking him into a hotel. It meant paying the hotel bill out of his own pocket.

The Samaritan didn't stop and figure out how much those things were going to cost him. Nor did he worry about protecting his own goods or complain about the guy getting blood all over his saddle. He didn't think about whether or not his Samaritan friends would approve of him getting involved with someone who "wasn't his kind."

Compassion is the opposite of the spirit of racism, strife and division. Compassion forgets about what's "mine" and just says, "I have to get the love of God to this person."

LITTLE THINGS CAN MAKE A BIG DIFFERENCE

Can you imagine what could happen if every one of us made the decision to live by compassion? We could turn the tables on racism and the devil so fast it would make his head spin! We could undercut the spirit of division in one way or another every day. We might not always have the opportunity to do something as dramatic as the Samaritan did, but dramatic actions aren't always needed. Sometimes, it's the little things that make the difference.

Years ago, I heard a minister give a testimony at an anti-drug rally in which Gloria and I were taking part. He told how as an unsaved teenager growing up in a rough area of Chicago, he once shot a white boy with a homemade pistol. "Please, mister! Please, mister!" his victim had cried as he lay bleeding on the ground, "Please don't shoot me again."

For a teenager who'd been treated with disrespect by every white man he'd ever known, hearing those words was like getting a shot of heroin. He was immediately addicted. As he put it, "When the kid I shot called me *Mister*, I made a life-altering decision to use violence to gain the respect I'd been denied for so long. I decided, *I'm going to get every white man I can in front of my gun.*"

At that point in the man's story, as I was sitting there in that rally, the compassion of God rose up in me. I thought, *If someone had just called that young man "Mister" and treated him with dignity, it could have changed the course of his life. He might not have decided to start shooting people.* Right then, I made a decision before God. I said, "LORD, from now on, when I interact with a young man or woman, I'm not going to refer to them as kids. I'm not going to call them just by their first names. I'm going to call them *Mister* or *Miss.*

You might think that's a bit extreme or ridiculous and think, *I'm not going to call some kid Mister.*

Compassion will.

Compassion will move you to do anything The LORD tells you to do that will make a young man feel a little better about himself. Compassion will move you to treat all young people the way God sees them—not as just a bunch of tattooed, pierced teenagers, but as young men and women who can walk in victory and power with God.

Compassion is the devil's worst nightmare! He can't overcome it.

I'm thinking right now, for example, about an extremely powerful turnaround that took place as a result of the compassion of my friend Joe Nanowski. He's gone home to be with The LORD now, but one time, many years ago, he was in Detroit for a convention. He was eating dinner in a restaurant, when he noticed a family seated at another table. Drawn to them by the love of The LORD, he stopped to chat with them after he finished his meal.

He nodded hello to the father and mother and their two little boys, and then said to the father, "I couldn't help but notice what a fine looking family you have, and I just thought I'd invite you all to the meeting we're having here tonight. We're going to be talking about Jesus, and you're more than welcome to come. Most of all though, I just wanted to tell you what a wonderful family you have."

Joe was the kind of man who was always laughing and loving people and having a good time. So while he was saying all this, he was teasing the two children by stealing french fries off their plates. They were giggling and enjoying the attention. As he left, he put his arms around both the little boys, hugged them, and told them he appreciated meeting them. That's all he did. It took less than five minutes. But as it turned out, five minutes of compassion can change everything.

The family went to the meeting that night and they all received Jesus as their Savior and were baptized in the Holy

Spirit. Afterward, the husband told Joe, "I had a loaded pistol in my pocket when you walked up to our table. My family didn't know it but that was going to be our final meal together. I'd had some bad dealings with a white lawyer whose office was right across the street from the restaurant, and I'd made up my mind that after dinner, I'd go over to his office, shoot him and then shoot myself."

"What caused you to change your mind?" Joe asked.

"Your eating french fries off my kids' plates," he answered.

"What did that have to do with it?"

"Up to that moment, I'd been convinced no white man cared anything at all about me. I thought I could settle the score by killing that lawyer and then myself. But when you came up and started playing with my kids and being so kind, something happened inside me. My heart just melted."

Think of it! The devil had been working on that man for years to drive him toward murder and suicide. He'd used the spirit of division and the ugliness of racism to hijack the man's destiny and put him on the road to hell. Yet, one act of compassion undid all the devil's hard work. It melted the hatred in that man, and set him and his entire family on a whole new course. The last I heard about him he was serving The LORD in full-time ministry.

That's what the power of compassion can do!

CHAPTER 5

DON'T TAKE THE BAIT

*Let nothing be done through strife or
vainglory; but in lowliness of mind let each
esteem other better than themselves. Look not
every man on his own things, but every man
also on the things of others.*

Philippians 2:3-4

Imagine if each of us made ourselves more available to God to do the kind of thing Joe Nanowski did. Think what could happen if believers everywhere reached out in compassion to people the way he reached out to that family at the restaurant. We could change lives everywhere we go.

To do that, however, most of us would have to make some adjustments in our way of thinking. We'd have to become more sensitive to what's going on with other people who come across our paths, less preoccupied with how things will affect us and more attentive to how things affect them.

As we've already seen, that's what the Samaritan did in Luke 10. When he encountered the man who'd been wounded on the roadside, he didn't just jerk the fellow up by the arm and send him on his way. He didn't ignore his cuts and bruises, slap him on the back and say, "Well, have a good day!" Instead, he was sensitive to the man's condition, taking the time to find out what had happened to him, what he needed, and then responding accordingly.

If we're going to bridge gaps that have been created by the spirit of division, we'll need to do the same. We'll need to care enough to put ourselves in the other fellow's shoes and find out how he thinks, so we can be the blessing we want to be. This is especially true where matters of race are concerned. If we don't understand how people of other skin colors or ethnicities see things, we can wind up saying and doing things that are offensive to them simply because we don't know any better. We can hurt them accidentally, just because we don't understand their point of view.

This happens all the time in the United States between different races. Sometimes, a white person will make a seemingly racist remark without having any idea he or she has said anything wrong. A black person, for example, will hear the remark and conclude the white person is a bigot who is intentionally trying to insult him or her. The black person will think, *No one could say something that insensitive without knowing exactly what he or she is doing, No one could be that ignorant!*

What the black person may not realize, however, is that those of us who grew up white in a predominantly white culture really *can* be that ignorant! Generally speaking, we weren't raised to give much thought to how people of other races perceive us.

Unlike most black Americans who faced prejudice from an early age and had to be attentive to learn how white people relate, white Americans haven't had that experience. They tend to be less aware of the racial implications of things they say. As a result, they can be offensive to people of different skin colors without even realizing it.

Such mistakes aren't unique to white people, of course. Everyone, regardless of skin color, can be offensive at times, so we shouldn't be hard on each other. If someone says something insensitive to us, we ought to believe the best and assume that person isn't intentionally trying to hurt us. Such assumptions are particularly safe in church because no born-again child of God can truly be a racist. No Christian, regardless of how he or she has been raised to think or talk about people of other races, can truly be a bigot at heart.

Bigotry, in the genuine sense, is an anointing from the devil. It's a hard, mean, demon-possessed condition. If you ever meet a *real* bigot, you'll never forget it. He can look at you and say, "Good morning," and it will turn your blood cold. You'll sense just being around him, there's a devil at work in him that would kill you if it got the chance.

One time when I was preaching at a prison, I met a man who'd been so possessed by bigotry that they put him in lockdown for 24 years. They had to keep him in solitary confinement because if he got close to a black man or a brown man, he'd murder him on the spot. Somehow, during his years in solitary, he got born again and filled with the Holy Spirit. The first time they ever let him out was when he came to hear me preach. During the meeting, he sat with a black man on one side and a brown man on the other. While I was preaching I went over there to him and said, "This is good stuff, isn't it!" He hugged the men sitting next to him, jumped straight up in the air and said, "Yeah, glory to God! This is the greatest stuff I ever heard in all my life!"

That man was a freer man in prison than he'd ever been as a hater out walking the streets. He not only loved Jesus, he loved those men he was sitting with. He wasn't a bigot anymore. He was still pretty rough around the edges, but his heart was right.

That's true about all believers, to some degree. We're all still a little rough in some areas. We're all in the process of learning how to be as sensitive to each other as we should be. But our hearts are right. We aren't bigots, so we don't have to react to each other on that basis. We can believe the best of each other and be gracious and forgiving when one of our brothers or sisters makes a racial blunder or says something insensitive.

At the same time though, we shouldn't be content to remain ignorant. We should pay attention and find out how to speak and behave in ways that minister life and compassion to people of other ethnicities and backgrounds. And, vice versa. All of us should learn to relate to each other in such a way that, if people have been hurt by the spirit of division, we can bring healing instead of causing them more pain.

How exactly do we learn to do this? It's simple, really. If you're white and you don't have much understanding about how black or brown, yellow or red people feel, go ask someone of those races to share their wisdom with you. If you're a member of a non-white race, go talk to someone who's white. Open yourself up to their input. Tell them you don't want to be unkind or hurt anyone, then give them permission to correct you if they hear you say something offensive. Be humble enough to let them help you become more sensitive.

TAKING CARE OF BUSINESS

But what about the people who actually do say offensive things on purpose? What if they know they're hurting others, and they don't care?

I'll tell you what The LORD told me about that many years ago. He said, *Whether or not other people care about you is none of your business. Your business is to care about them. Your business is to have compassion on them and refuse to take offense.*

No matter how offensive people might be, you must never, for any reason, allow yourself to become offended with them. It's not worth it. When they say something ugly to you, and you react in anger and strife, you give power to their negative words. Their words become *your* problem because you've agreed with them. You've received what they said. By taking offense, you've become a partner with them and opened yourself up to the work of the devil. You've given the spirit of division permission to work in your house, and you're about to start going down because a house divided cannot stand.

Don't get caught in that trap! What difference does it make what anyone else says about you? According to Mark 11:23, you have what *you* say, not what *they* say.

I found out years ago that people can call me whatever they want, and it won't affect me at all—unless I let it. You can call me a poor, old, fat, dumb preacher, and I won't even get upset. I'll just choose not to answer to it. I'll keep right on believing and confessing the truth: that I'm BLESSED, smart, prosperous and good-looking!

On the other hand, if I see I can be of help to you, I'll respond in love and say, "What can I do for you? How can I BLESS you?"

Personally, I like taking that kind of attitude toward offensive people because even if it doesn't do anything to help them, it stops me from getting entangled in the trash they're dishing out. It keeps me free from strife so I can respond with compassion and pray, *Lord, help those people. They really need Jesus. Or, maybe their brains have just overheated!*

One of the Partners of this ministry shared with me how he took this approach one time during a labor dispute at his company. While the meetings were going on, instead of taking part in the fight, he just sat there praying silently in the

Holy Spirit. He just kept binding the devil and loving everyone. The meetings dragged on for days without producing any resolution, and as the arguments between management and labor grew more heated, the atmosphere became more volatile. (As our Partner put it, "It was a good thing no one was carrying a gun!") Eventually, the two sides were practically at each other's throats.

About the time it looked as if they were going to destroy the company, our Partner noticed another fellow sitting across the room from him and sensed he was praying, too. He got the fellow's attention and they moved closer together so they could talk. "Do I know you?" our Partner asked.

"No, I don't think you do," the fellow responded. "But it seems like I know you in The LORD."

As it turned out, one of them was with labor and the other with management. So, they got busy exchanging ideas about possible solutions to the mess and writing them down. Without anyone noticing, they sat there and worked out a deal. Once they got it put together, all of a sudden, everyone else in the room just got quiet and looked at them. "Do you have something to say?" someone asked. "Yes, we do," they answered. Laying out the plan The LORD had helped them come up with, they brought both sides together and everyone got in agreement. A new contract was written, and the company was saved!

DON'T GIVE THE DEVIL ANY REAL ESTATE IN YOUR LIFE

But you might be thinking: *Even though I know I should take the high road and refuse to take offense, sometimes when people hurt my feelings I'm not willing to let them off the hook that easily.*

You'd be willing if you understood how much keeping them *on* the hook will cost you in the undermining of your faith and stopping The WORD of God from operating in your life. As shocking as it sounds, that's exactly what offense will do. Jesus confirmed it in the parable of the sower when He said:

> The sower soweth The WORD. And these are they by the way side, where The WORD is sown; but when they have heard, Satan cometh immediately, and taketh away The WORD that was sown in their

hearts. And these are they likewise which are sown on stony ground; who, when they have heard The WORD, immediately receive it with gladness; and have no root in themselves, and so endure but for a time: afterward, when affliction or persecution ariseth for The WORD's sake, immediately *they are offended*. And these are they which are sown among thorns; such as hear The WORD, and the cares of this world, and the deceitfulness of riches, and the lusts of other things entering in, choke The WORD, and it becometh unfruitful. And these are they which are sown on good ground; such as hear The WORD, and receive it, and bring forth fruit, some thirtyfold, some sixty, and some an hundred (Mark 4:14-20, italics mine).

You can see how serious the taking of offense is by looking at verse 17 in the *The Amplified Bible, Classic Edition*. "When trouble or persecution arises on account of The WORD, they immediately are offended (become displeased, indignant, resentful) and they stumble and fall away." Stumbling and falling away from The WORD is costly business! It puts you in a place where you can't receive the covenant blessings God has provided for you.

If you've ever fallen away from The WORD by trading it for a costly case of offense (and who hasn't?), you know how it usually happens. You go to church or a wonderful meeting somewhere, hear The WORD preached, and go home rejoicing. Faith rises up in you, and you're on your way to new levels of victory. Then a few days later, some spirit-of-division-inspired person comes along and rails on you about something, and you take the devil's bait. You stop thinking about The WORD you heard and start thinking, instead, about the ugly things that person said to you: *He (or she) has no right to say such mean things to me! That hurt my feelings!*

For a while, you resist the offense. You try to forget about it, and the devil accommodates you by leaving you alone for a little while. He lets you settle down because he doesn't want you to figure out he's there. But after a while, or in the middle of the night, you wake up and, once again, find yourself thinking, *I wonder why he said that about me? I'm a nice person! I ought to give him a dose of his own medicine just to see how he likes it!*

This is the main way the devil operates. It's one of his primary ploys, and if you fall for it, he'll use it to take you for everything you've got. He'll use it to steal The WORD from you—your healing, your prosperity, your protection, the deliverance of your family and everything else he can get his hands on.

So don't fall for it! Reject offense at every turn. Make a quality decision to do what Ephesians 4:27 says: "Neither give place to the devil"!

According to a friend who's a Greek scholar, the words *"neither give place to the devil"* carry a lot of force in the original language. They indicate the Apostle Paul was practically shouting, "STOP IT! STOP GIVING THE DEVIL A PLACE!" The word *place,* which is translated from the Greek word *topos,* speaks of topography or an exact location. It brings to mind the kind of topographical map that's so detailed it shows everything about a piece of property. It shows how high the hills are and what the terrain is like. It has everything on it but the grasshoppers.

The devil is looking at that kind of map of your life. He's scouring every detail to see if he can find a place where he can gain entrance. He's searching for a piece of real estate from which he can launch an attack. Living up to his name (which means *agitator* or *slanderer)* he irritates, pokes, presses and pecks at you, trying to force his way into your affairs. He pokes at you through your family and through the television. He gripes at you, irritates and harasses you any way he can.

What's he doing? He's trying to find a handle. He's trying to locate a touchy place in you that will make you react in anger and offense. The minute he finds it and you step out into his territory, he'll move in. He'll take advantage of that little sore spot and keep injecting it with the poison of offense until, like a splinter festering in your finger, it becomes increasingly infected.

No wonder Paul was shouting, "STOP IT!" If you give the devil a place, he will inject so much offense into you, it will destroy you. What's worse, he won't stop with you, he'll start using you to inject that poison into the lives of others. He'll follow you around and use your hurt feelings and resentments to drive people apart instead of bringing them together. One day, you'll look around and find division breaking out everywhere you go. You'll realize the spirit of division has begun to use you to do his dirty work in your family, at your place of employment and even in your church. And that, as we say in Texas, "opens up a whole nother can of worms"!

CHAPTER 6

STRIFE-FREE AND STANDING TALL

*But if ye have bitter envying and strife in
your hearts, glory not, and lie not against
the truth. This wisdom descendeth not from
above, but is earthly, sensual, devilish.
For where envying and strife is, there is
confusion and every evil work.*

James 3:14-16

The first time I got an up-close look at a group of believers who'd been infected by the poison of division happened not long after I was born again. A local pastor who knew I was a pilot called me and said, "Kenneth, I have a meeting at a church out in West Texas this evening, and I have to be back home by tonight. If I rent a plane, could you fly me out there?" I told him I could, assuming he was just going to preach. But I soon discovered he'd actually been called in to arbitrate a dispute that had broken out in the congregation. The dispute was so bitter, it was threatening to split the church.

When we arrived, the place was packed. Almost the entire congregation, it seemed, had turned out for the meeting. (People might skip a Sunday morning service, but they'll always show up for a fight!) The groups on either side of the argument had divided up and were fuming at each other from opposite sides of the auditorium. The pastor I'd flown out there opened the meeting and began asking questions to find out how it had all started, but no one seemed to know.

I was just a spiritual novice, fresh off the street, so I didn't have any experience with church fights. But as I watched the conflict unfold, I noticed one man, in particular, kept stirring things up. Whenever the pastor made some headway toward bringing the two sides together, he'd start raising objections. He'd stand up and say, "Now, wait just a minute!" Then he'd rehearse his list of offenses.

As the evening wore on, my patience wore thin. *If someone would shut that fellow up, we could get this argument resolved and go home,* I thought. Looking at the pastor, I could tell he was as concerned as I was about how long all this was taking, so I started coming up with a plan. I figured I could ease up next to the troublemaker and tell him he was needed outside, or something. Then I could follow him out, spank him a little, and send him on home!

It didn't occur to me that The LORD might object to such tactics. But just as I was about to carry out my mission, something unexpected happened. The guy suddenly got mad and walked out of the meeting. Thinking back on it now, I'm fully convinced he left because the spirit of division had picked up on what I was about to do. The devil realized I was about to bounce the guy and got him out of there. After all, the man was working for him, and he wanted to protect his agitator!

Proverbs 22:10 says when you "cast out the scorner...contention shall go out; yea, strife and reproach shall cease." I saw it proven that night. It was amazing how things changed once that man was out of the building. The strife disappeared, and the place just got lovely. Everyone just started getting along. They couldn't remember why they'd been so angry. They began talking to each other and, before long, they were saying, "Let's just put these disagreements behind us!"

After the meeting was over, the pastor and I were in the airplane flying home, and I told him what I'd been planning to do. "You know, just before that guy left, I was about to drag him outside and put a stop to that stuff," I said.

"Why didn't you?" he replied. "Why'd you wait so long?" He was joking, of course. Being older in The LORD than I was, he knew better than to slap someone around. But he momentarily enjoyed the thought!

STRIFE AND DIVISION WILL MAKE YOU EASY PREY

In the years I've been in ministry I've seen similar things happen time and again. I've witnessed firsthand how the spirit of division can tear up the Body of Christ. I've also learned just how much The LORD disapproves of such situations. Strife is at the top of the list of things He despises. He literally hates it when someone sows "discord among brethren" (Proverbs 6:19).

What makes it so unacceptable? It stops THE BLESSING from functioning, and it empowers the curse. It puts us in the same position in which the Israelites found themselves during the battle at Ai. If you've read the story, you probably remember what happened in that battle. The Israelites experienced a military meltdown. They suffered a devastating defeat at the hands of a rag-tag little army they should have easily beaten.

The Israelites lost that easy battle! Their leader, Joshua, was so upset when he heard about it that he tore his clothes, fell down on the ground, and said:

O LORD, what shall I say, when Israel turneth their backs before their enemies! For the Canaanites and all the inhabitants of the land shall hear of it, and shall environ us round, and cut off our name from the earth: and what wilt thou do unto thy great name? And The LORD said unto Joshua, Get thee up; wherefore liest thou thus upon thy face? Israel hath sinned, and they have also transgressed my covenant which I commanded them: for they have even taken of the accursed thing…. Therefore the children of Israel could not stand before their enemies…. Up, sanctify the people, and say, Sanctify yourselves against to morrow: for thus saith The LORD God of Israel, There is an accursed thing in the midst of thee, O Israel: thou canst not stand before thine enemies, until ye take away the accursed thing from among you (Joshua 7:8-13).

Take a close look at that last verse. It reveals exactly why the Israelites lost the battle at Ai. They had an "accursed thing" in their midst. It stopped THE BLESSING from operating and weakened them so much, they couldn't stand against their enemies.

You're in bad shape when you can't stand against your enemies! You're in trouble when God tells you, as He did in Ephesians 6:11, to "stand against the wiles of the devil," but you suddenly find you're *unable* to stand. When that happens, you're about to become easy prey for your adversary the devil, who "walks about like a roaring lion, seeking whom he may devour" (1 Peter 5:8, *New King James Version)*. He's going to see your strife-weakened condition and come after you. He's going to beat you like the army of Ai beat the Israelites.

The reason strife and division—in a family, a church, a community, a nation—is such a big deal to God is because it's in direct violation of the one commandment we, as New Testament believers, have been given by The LORD. It's a violation of the law of love. Strife is the exact opposite of the lay-down-your-life-for-each-other kind of compassion Jesus told us to walk in. It's a manifestation of selfishness and hate.

If you doubt it, just look at what Proverbs says:

- "Hatred stirreth up strifes: but love covereth all sins" (Proverbs 10:12).

- "A wrathful man stirreth up strife: but he that is slow to anger appeaseth strife" (Proverbs 15:18).

- "A froward man soweth strife: and a whisperer separateth chief friends" (Proverbs 16:28).

- "An angry man stirreth up strife, and a furous man aboundeth in transgression" (Proverbs 29:22).

- "He that is of a proud heart stirreth up strife: but he that putteth his trust in The LORD shall be made fat" (Proverbs 28:25).

Notice, Proverbs 28:25 contrasts the person who's in strife with someone who's "made fat." One of the Old Testament meanings of the word *fat,* in this verse, is "to anoint."[10] So the person who trusts The LORD shall be *anointed*—and the person who stirs up strife will not be anointed!

As we've already seen, that's something the Christians in Corinth found out. They argued and fought away their anointing until they got to the point where they couldn't understand spiritual things anymore. What Jesus warned about in the parable of the sower happened in a major way

---

10 "fat," *The New Strong's Exhaustive Concordance of the Bible* (Nashville: Thomas Nelson, 1984) H1878.

to the Corinthian believers. They became offended with one another, and that spirit of offense robbed them of their revelation of The WORD. They became such spiritual babies again that the Apostle Paul had to write to them and say: "And I, brethren, could not speak unto you as unto spiritual, but as unto carnal, even as unto babes in Christ. I have fed you with milk, and not with meat: for hitherto ye were not able to bear it, neither yet now are ye able. For ye are yet carnal: for whereas there is among you envying, and strife, and divisions, are ye not carnal, and walk as men?" (1 Corinthians 3:1-3). *The Amplified Bible, Classic Edition* says, "...are you not unspiritual and of the flesh, behaving yourselves after a human standard and like mere (unchanged) men?" The most anointed teacher since Jesus could not break through the strife barrier.

LITTLE WORDS CAN START BIG FIRES

As Christians, it's essential that we are able to understand The WORD of God and hear the voice of The LORD in our spirits. We can't live a successful Christian life without those things, but, according to 1 Corinthians 3:1-3, strife robs us of them.

What's more, strife hangs around with very bad company. The New Testament calls it a "work of the flesh" and lists it with such things as: adultery, fornication, uncleanness, lasciviousness, idolatry, witchcraft, hatred, variance, emulations, wrath, seditions, heresies, envyings, murders, drunkenness and revellings (Galatians 5:19-21). Most of us have enough sense to run from those kinds of things. We don't pal around with people who live in adultery or practice witchcraft, and we don't buddy up with murderers or drunkards.

We should have the same attitude about strife and division carriers and people who spread offense. We should turn a deaf ear or just walk away when someone comes up to us at church and says something like, "You know I love Pastor, right? But I've been watching him lately and it seems to me he's giving certain people in this church preferential treatment. I mean, I don't want to accuse him of prejudice or anything, but I've been wondering what's really behind some of the decisions he's been making."

That kind of talk leads to strife and it will bring THE BLESSING to a screeching halt in our lives! It will mess us up before we even realize what's happening. We don't have any business judging other people's motives and decisions—much less gossiping about them. The minute we catch ourselves doing it, we should stop and repent on the spot, right in front of the person we're talking to.

The WORD of God tells us "foolish and unlearned questions avoid, knowing that they do gender strifes." It says, "The servant of The LORD *must not strive...*" (2 Timothy 2:23-24). Notice, those verses don't say strife is OK sometimes. They say we must *not* engage in it. Do you understand *must not?* It means never, ever do it. Instead, we're to "be gentle unto all men, apt to teach, patient, in meekness instructing those that oppose themselves [or get into strife]; if God peradventure will give them repentance to the acknowledging of the truth; and that they may recover themselves out of the snare of the devil, who are taken captive by him at his will" (verses 24-26).

You may think a few words spoken when you're upset can't cause that much trouble, but according to the book of James, words of strife work like kindling. They seem small, but they start big fires.

If you're familiar with fire-building, you know you can't start a big bonfire just by sticking a match under a log. Big logs don't burn that easily. You have to gather up some brush or little, dry sticks and use them as kindling to ignite the rest of the wood. One of the best sources of kindling is an old pine-tree stump. The sap in those stumps turns into a form of turpentine that's extremely flammable. If you dig a few sticks out of a pine stump, you can put a match to them, and they'll burn instantly. They'll start a blaze that, if you keep stoking it, will get bigger…and bigger…and bigger.

The Apostle James wrote: "Behold, how great a matter a little fire kindleth! And the tongue is a fire, a world of iniquity: so is the tongue among our members, that it defileth the whole body, and setteth on fire the course of nature; and it is set on fire of hell" (James 3:5-6).

Words can light fires that will absolutely destroy people's lives! They can kindle a bonfire so big that no natural force can stop it. The tongue is what ignites the fire. It's what starts breaking up the marriage before you even know it's in danger. It's what puts things in your life on a downhill slide.

The power of death and life is in the tongue (Proverbs 18:21). If the devil can get your tongue, nothing in your life is safe. You can spend hours and days and years building your faith in The WORD. You can confess that you're blessed, every hour of every day. But if you start fires of strife with your mouth, those fires will eventually burn up the good things THE BLESSING brings your way. And, if you don't repent, one of these days, you'll find yourself sitting in an ash heap wondering what hit you.

How can you make sure that doesn't happen to you?

First Corinthians 11:28 says, "Let a man examine himself...." Spend some time with The LORD and ask Him to reveal to you any offenses you might be harboring. You may be surprised at what you discover. He may show you that, while you're not in strife with any of your friends or family members, maybe you've been offended at the president. You might realize you've been in strife with people of differing political viewpoints, denominations, people of another race or religion. You don't have to be acquainted with someone to be offended with them. You can be in strife all by yourself with people you don't even know.

When you examine yourself before The LORD, if you identify some areas where you've been in strife, don't condemn yourself over it. Condemnation doesn't change anything. You can beat yourself over the head for the rest of your life for doing something wrong, and it won't change a thing. All it will do is make your head sore! So just skip the condemnation, go to God and repent.

The word *repent* means "to change direction." So turn around, and go the other way. Where you've been thinking, talking and acting in offense, stop it—immediately. Don't just think to yourself, *I'll start working on it.* (What does that mean—you'll just get mad twice a day now, instead of five times?) No, you don't *work on* sin, you renounce it and get it out of your life!

Many people say they've tried and haven't been able to do that. They keep repenting, but the feelings of offense just keep coming back.

The answer to that is to quit focusing on your feelings. Focus instead on 1 John 1:9 that says, "If we confess our sins, he is faithful and just to forgive us our sins, and to cleanse us from all unrighteousness." That verse will set you free every time! It never fails. So act on it by faith. Believe and receive the forgiveness it provides and the cleansing it promises. Instead of saying, "I can't do it!" start saying, "Thank God, I'm delivered from offense. I am not in strife anymore. I'm free from it, in the Name of Jesus."

If feelings of offense keep pestering you for a while, choose to not let them move you. Just keep speaking the truth about it—what God's WORD says about it. Instead of thinking, *Well, I thought I was delivered, but I guess I'm not,* say, "I'm not moved by feelings. God says in 1 John 1:9 that if I confess my sins, He is faithful and just to forgive me and to cleanse me from ALL unrighteousness. So I say, by faith in God's WORD, that I'm cleansed of offense, and I believe it. I'm living a strife-free life because I can do all things through Christ which strengthens me!"

The more you talk this way, the stronger it will get inside you, until when the opportunity to get into strife comes up again (and it will), you'll be on immediate alert, and you won't take the devil's bait.

CHAPTER 7

SITUATIONAL AWARENESS

Starting a quarrel is like opening a floodgate,
so stop before a dispute breaks out.

Proverbs 17:14,
New Living Translation

Pilots who want to stay out of trouble must develop an extremely high level of situational awareness. With planes flying faster and faster, it's not enough anymore to just "kick tires and light fires" (as they used to say more than 50 years ago when I first became a pilot). It's not even enough to know how to operate the systems in the aircraft. When you're flying at speeds of up to 600 miles per hour or more, you have to be acutely aware of everything that's going on in and around you while you're in the cockpit. You have to pay attention to your every thought and every word. You must be aware of every blinking light, every number that comes up on the panel, and everything that's happening with your crew. If you aren't, you can get in trouble fast. You can just be bumbling along in your own little world assuming things are fine, and suddenly find yourself in the midst of a full-blown crisis.

Spiritually, the same principle applies to us as believers. Especially these days, as we're moving faster and faster toward the return of The LORD Jesus, we have to be constantly alert. If we want to stay on course and deal effectively with everything the spirit of division throws at us, we must be situationally aware, or things can quickly start going wrong.

We can slip into strife and be in trouble before we know what's happening.

You know what I'm talking about. You might be having lunch with your co-workers one day and, suddenly, the conversation takes an unexpected turn. Someone starts griping about the stupid decisions the supervisor has been making and, before you know it, everyone else is piling on unflattering stories about the guy. For a while, you don't say anything. You just sit there listening, as nice as can be, but on the inside you're getting riled up. You're picking up their offenses. Later in the day, you're back at work, and before you realize what you're doing, you repeat to someone else the ugly things you heard at lunch. You spout off about that supervisor and damage his reputation.

The same kind of scenario can even take place at church. You might be talking with a group of other believers after the service when somehow the subject of politics comes up. Someone brings up a politician you don't particularly like and says, "You know, that guy claims to be a Christian, but I've heard he's had a lot of extramarital affairs. Even the media reported on it." With your opinion of the guy confirmed, you go off, filled with righteous indignation and end up repeating that rumor a number of times before you find out it's totally false.

What could possibly make you say such ugly things when you're so committed to steering clear of strife and keeping your foot on the neck of the spirit of division? Lack of situational awareness. You weren't alert to the warning signs, so strife was able to sneak up on you.

You may think you can just go back later and apologize, but apologies don't necessarily undo the damage. Bitter words are like "arrows," Psalm 64:3 says. Or, in today's vernacular, they're like bullets. So, by the time you make your apologies, someone has already been "shot." You may feel bad about it and say something like, "I so apologize for letting my mouth go off like a machine gun! I just regret that I "shot" so many people before I could get it under control!"

But, your bitter words can't be taken back. Once you've released them and they've hit their mark, someone, somewhere is bleeding and hurting.

When you're spiritually aware, however, you'll catch yourself before you do that kind of damage. You'll notice the thoughts you're thinking *before* you speak them, and pick up on it when the spirit of division is trying to get a foothold. Spiritual awareness will help you keep your mouth shut the moment you sense the first stirrings of offense, until you've dealt with whatever is bothering you.

That's always the wisest course of action. It's best to shut the devil down before he can get anything going. As Proverbs 17:14 says, "The beginning of strife is as when water first trickles [from a crack in a dam]; therefore stop contention before it becomes worse and quarreling breaks out" *(The Amplified Bible, Classic Edition).*

ROOFERS, PLUMBERS AND DOCTRINAL DISPUTES

Most arguments we get into aren't worth the effort, anyway. From what I've seen, especially in churches, when people get into strife, it's usually just because of a misunderstanding. Often it's even because we have different callings in the Body of Christ. Some believers are called to major on evangelism, for instance, so they're convinced the only thing that matters is sharing the gospel with the lost. Others are called to major on spiritual growth, so they think the Church's top priority should be teaching believers and helping them grow to maturity. A third group of believers might be called to major on the gifts of the Spirit, so they put the emphasis on learning to move with the Holy Spirit.

Which group is right? They all are. Each is focusing on what God has called them to do—and that's a wonderful thing! The only problem is, they don't always understand how they fit together. As a result, the spirit of division gets a foothold and starts tearing them apart.

The believer with an evangelical bent may find himself in a church that has a teaching bent and decides that everyone there is off base. He starts stirring up strife by bad-mouthing the Bible classes the pastor has been teaching. "Those classes are a waste of time!" he'll say. "This congregation ought to be on the street winning souls every night. I'm going to meet with Pastor and get his priorities straightened out!"

Across town, there's a church called to emphasize the gifts of the Holy Spirit, and one of their members who has a teaching bent is stirring up the same kind of trouble. He's complaining about their services. If someone moves in the gifts of the Spirit during a Sunday morning service, he's upset and criticizes the pastor for letting such a thing happen.

What we need to realize is that building the house of God is much like building a natural house. While everyone involved in the construction process is working toward the same overall goal, different groups have different assignments. Metaphorically speaking, one church might be a roofing church and another might be a plumbing church. Both roofing and plumbing are important. The house won't be complete without them. But, if one of the plumbers gets out of his place and goes over to the roofing church, he won't like anything about it. He'll be trying to install a toilet on the roof and won't understand why his pastor isn't in favor of it. Over time, the devil will keep stoking the division and magnifying the differences between the believer and his pastor, until everyone's miserable.

What's the solution?

Again, it's situational awareness. If we're aware of what God has called us to do, we can go to Him when things start rubbing us the wrong way and find out what the problem is. Then, instead of getting into strife, we can maintain peace by making adjustments as The LORD leads.

In the situation where the plumbing believer is in a roofing church, the pastor might call that believer and say, "I'd like to be a blessing to you, and it seems you're upset by the way we do things here. I love you, and I think you might be happier with a pastor who thinks more like you do. I know one who fits that description, and if you'd like, I'll set up a time for us all to go out to lunch together. You can meet him, and if your heart bears witness, you can go on over there to his church."

When we take that approach and refuse to give place to the spirit of division, it doesn't matter how different we are from each other, we can resolve conflicts in a way that strengthens rather than weakens the Body of Christ. We can work together and stop getting into strife. We can keep right on loving and get along with each other—even when we disagree on doctrinal issues.

Many believers might insist doctrinal differences are important and should be staunchly embraced and strongly defended. But, we don't need to get into strife over them!

You might not believe a word I preach, and I might not agree with a word you preach, but we don't have to get mad at each other over it. We don't have to let the devil steal The WORD out of our hearts by causing us to be offended with one another. We can just agree to disagree. We can each honor the other's freedom to believe what he or she chooses.

I know it can be done because I've done it many times. I got into a discussion one time, for example, with a fellow who claimed that Jesus was an American Indian. "I can prove it to you from the Bible!" he insisted. I asked him for a specific scripture reference and he cited Ephesians 2:20. "That verse identifies Jesus as Chief Cornerstone!" he said.

Talk about a wild way to interpret a scripture. That beat anything I'd ever heard, but I didn't jump on the guy about it. I'm glad I didn't, too, because in that particular case, it turned out he was kidding. But what if he hadn't been? What if he'd really believed it? As far as I'm concerned, that would be his prerogative. He can go to bed every night of his life worshiping Chief Cornerstone if he wants to, and I'll still smile at him every time I see him. I'll speak the truth to him in love, and if he's interested, I'll offer to show him what the Bible really says about the issue. I'll let him know that, even though it would thrill me to find out that Jesus is really Cherokee (because that's my family background), the reality is, He's Jewish!

Whatever happens, though, I won't argue with the fellow because I don't want us to be divided. I want us growing up together in love. I don't want some stupid squabble to turn us into spiritual "children, tossed to and fro, and carried about with every wind of doctrine, by the sleight of men, and cunning craftiness, whereby they lie in wait to deceive" (Ephesians 4:14).

Deception is an ugly thing, and it walks hand in hand with the spirit of division. When we fight with one another and start dividing up, some con man will always be out there waiting to deceive us. Why? Because when we're in strife, we don't have much spiritual aptitude. We can become easy marks for any shady character the devil sends our way.

THE LEVEL OF THE BODY AFFECTS EVERY INDIVIDUAL IN IT

The devil will use strife to rob entire churches. If we allow him to, he'll deceive us into arguing and dividing from one another on such a broad scale that it can cost us all!

I saw a prime example of this many years ago when The LORD

gave me a mandate to share with the rest of the Body of Christ what He was showing me about finances: *I'm going to teach you the laws that govern prosperity and abundance,* He said, *and I'm going to hold you responsible for the revelation of it.* I did exactly what He said to do. I began teaching on the laws of prosperity. But before long, something bizarre happened.

Preachers started calling me and chewing me out because I wouldn't borrow money and get into debt. Ugly debates began to rage over whether or not it really was God's will for His people to live debt-free and walk in financial abundance. Finally, God said to me one day in prayer, *Don't teach on the laws of prosperity anymore until I tell you.*

"Why not?" I asked.

There's strife in the camp. Other preachers are mad at you and offended over it.

"But LORD!" I protested, "I don't understand this. If I were preaching the new birth and they were mad about it, You wouldn't let me back off. Why are you telling me to back off from this?"

Prospering financially and in the material realm is a privilege,

He answered. *If they don't want to hear it, they'll just have to do without.*

It made sense, and I didn't think much about it at the time. But had I known then what I know now, I wouldn't have taken it so calmly. I'd have interceded night and day and done everything I knew to change the situation, but I wasn't aware of what was about to happen. I didn't realize that this situation would affect us all. But, that's the way this works. When the rest of the Body of Christ put on the brakes in the area of prosperity, it slowed me down as well—particularly, when it came to the revelations The LORD had given me that I hadn't yet preached. When I tried to walk them out myself, I couldn't seem to do it.

Eventually, I asked The LORD, "Is there something wrong with me?"

No, you're just bumping into a spiritual reality, He said. *The maturity level of the whole Body affects every individual in it.* (See 1 Corinthians 12:14-16.) Then, He reminded me of what happened to Joshua and Caleb in the Old Testament.

If ever there were two men of great faith, it was Joshua and

Caleb. They stood on The WORD of God and said, "Let's take the Promised Land! God has delivered our enemies into our hands!" But the rest of the Israelites said, "No way. We can't do it. We're grasshoppers in their eyes." (See Numbers 13-14.) So what happened? Joshua and Caleb ended up wandering around in the wilderness with that unbelieving crowd until everyone over 20 years old, but them, died off.

Back in the early 1990s I saw this same spiritual principle go to work again when some well-known preachers stumbled in their walk with God. Believers all across the United States were offended, and instead of staying in faith and love, they began judging one another. For a while, it seemed Christians were gossiping and saying bad things about each other everywhere you turned—in the newspapers, on the radio, on television and even at church!

At our ministry, we kept our mouths shut. We weren't talking badly about anyone. In fact, we were saying good things to counter all the negative, trying to put a stop to it. But it affected us, anyway. It affected the scope of our ministry and our finances. Even though we didn't participate in all the mud-slinging, we suffered right along with the rest of the Body of Christ.

It was appalling to see the repercussions as that spirit of division and offense swept the land. Little country churches had their finances cut off. Missionaries suffered because of it. Eventually, believers began to see what was happening. The Church as a whole woke up and started realizing, "We'd better quit this. We'd better get our Bibles out, get back in The WORD, and quit destroying each other." By then, however, a lot of damage had already been done.

In these last days, as we move rapidly toward the coming of The LORD, we can't afford to let ourselves get into that kind of strife and division. We must rise above it by raising our level of spiritual awareness and being alert to the fact that as believers, we're not islands unto ourselves—we're part of a Body.

As Ephesians 4:16 says, we're "knit together by what every joint supplies" *(New King James Version)*. We're joined together by God, but we're held together by one another. I can't do anything without affecting you, and you can't do anything without affecting me because we're covenanted together in the blood of Jesus. When we accepted Him, we inherited one another.

We can't finish what God has called us to do on this planet

by living as individuals unto ourselves. We can only do it by growing up and working together. So, let's get after it! Let's pay attention spiritually to every thought we think and every word we say. Let's grow up together, speaking the truth [The WORD] to one another in love "till we all come in the unity of the faith, and of the knowledge of the Son of God, unto a perfect man, unto the measure of the stature of the fulness of Christ" (Ephesians 4:13).

CHAPTER 8

THE UNSTOPPABLE
FORCE OF FORGIVENESS

*Jesus said to them again, "Peace to you! As
the Father has sent Me, I also send you."
And when He had said this, He breathed
on them, and said to them, "Receive the
Holy Spirit. If you forgive the sins of any,
they are forgiven them; if you retain the
sins of any, they are retained.*

*John 20:21-23,
New King James Version*

J ust before I started this book, The LORD told me to do something I'd never done before. He told me to make a forgiveness list on which to include not only those who've wronged me personally, but people I wouldn't normally think to forgive. I was to forgive politicians, for instance, whose rhetoric and decisions have negatively affected our nation. I was also to consciously forgive people in places of influence who are yielding to the devil's pressure and doing things contrary to the will of God.

I had never thought of making that kind of list before, but I could immediately see the value of it. I knew from The WORD that walking in forgiveness should be a consistent part of our lifestyle as believers. The LORD even showed me a number of years ago that instead of waiting until someone does something ugly to me to forgive them, I can release forgiveness toward people all the time. For some time now, I've made it a practice, as I go about my day, to pray, "LORD, I forgive everyone around me, right now. I forgive everyone in the restaurant where I'm about to have lunch, and in all the places of business I go into today. In the Name of Jesus, I forgive everyone I encounter, everywhere I go."

Once I've prayed that way, I'm ready for any situation. Nothing anyone does can bother me because I forgave them before they ever did it. What's more, their hearts will be more open to hear my witness, and I can minister to them more effectively, because forgiveness brings God's supernatural power onto the scene.

"What does forgiveness have to do with the supernatural power of God?" you might ask.

It has everything to do with it! You can see that by looking at Jesus. During His earthly ministry, He operated in a constant flow of forgiveness. That's why the sin in people's lives never stopped them from getting healed or receiving a miracle from Him. His forgiveness moved their sin out of the way.

Think about what happened in Mark 2:5-12, for example, when the four men brought their paralyzed friend to Jesus. They couldn't get into the house where He was preaching because there were too many people inside. So, they went up on the roof, ripped a hole in it, and lowered their paralyzed friend down through the hole into the meeting.

> When Jesus saw their faith, he said unto the sick of the palsy, Son, thy sins be forgiven thee. But

there was certain of the scribes sitting there, and reasoning in their hearts, Why doth this man thus speak blasphemies? who can forgive sins but God only? And immediately when Jesus perceived in his spirit that they so reasoned within themselves, he said unto them, Why reason ye these things in your hearts? Whether is it easier to say to the sick of the palsy, Thy sins be forgiven thee; or to say, Arise, and take up thy bed, and walk? But that ye may know that the Son of man hath power on earth to forgive sins, (he saith to the sick of the palsy,) I say unto thee, Arise, and take up thy bed, and go thy way into thine house. And immediately he arose, took up the bed, and went forth before them all; insomuch that they were all amazed, and glorified God, saying, We never saw it on this fashion.

Notice, the first thing Jesus did there was to tell the man his sins were forgiven. When the scribes said He didn't have the power to provide such forgiveness, He showed them He did by healing the man. What does that prove? It proves the power that *forgives* is exactly the same power that heals.

Let me repeat that: The power that forgives is exactly the same power that heals! The Bible calls that power the *anointing*, and it's a tangible, spiritual force.

The anointing is the force that empowered Jesus to go about "doing good, and healing all that were oppressed of the devil" (Acts 10:38). It's the force He pointed to in Luke 4:18, when He said, "The Spirit of The LORD is upon me, because he hath *anointed* me to preach the gospel to the poor; he hath sent me to heal the brokenhearted, to preach deliverance to the captives, and recovering of sight to the blind, to set at liberty them that are bruised." It's the force the Prophet Isaiah was referring to when he said, "And it shall come to pass in that day, that [the enemy's] burden shall be taken away from off thy shoulder, and his yoke from off thy neck, and the yoke shall be destroyed because of the *anointing*" (Isaiah 10:27).

Talk about an unstoppable force! The *anointing* is the manifestation of the burden-removing, yoke-destroying power of Almighty God Himself—and it's the force behind forgiveness.

TICKED OFF? JUST PUT ANOTHER NAME ON YOUR LIST!

It's no wonder God told me to make a forgiveness list. When it comes to winning the war against the spirit of division, forgiveness is one of the mightiest weapons in our spiritual arsenal. As believers, we need to be using it all the time. We should even use it when we're watching TV. I was reminded of this not long ago when Gloria and I were watching a news broadcast and someone said something that really aggravated me. I was about to gripe and mouth off about the person, when I heard The LORD in my spirit say: *You can't be trusted with a news broadcast!*

My first impulse was to justify myself—*But LORD, did You hear what that guy just said?* But instead, I just repented and asked The LORD to forgive me. Then I picked up the remote, turned off the news, and switched over to the Believer's Voice of Victory Network on DISH˚.

A day or two later, I repeated the whole scenario. I turned on the news and got mad all over again. After I repented and acknowledged that I apparently still couldn't be trusted with a news broadcast, I heard The LORD: *Why don't you add that fellow on the news to your list?*

The LORD wants us to pray for those in authority, otherwise He wouldn't have told us in 1 Timothy 2:1-4:

> I exhort therefore, that, first of all, supplications, prayers, intercessions, and giving of thanks, be made for all men; for kings, and for all that are in authority; that we may lead a quiet and peaceable life in all godliness and honesty. For this is good and acceptable in the sight of God our Saviour; who will have all men to be saved, and to come unto the knowledge of the truth.

Look again at that last verse. It says God wants *all* men to come to the saving knowledge of Jesus. He doesn't want just the people in America to know Him. He doesn't want just the people we understand and agree with to know Him. He wants *every* politician and newscaster to know Him. He wants people of every tribe, tongue, nation and religion—including every terrorist—to know Him.

As John 3:16 says, God loves the *whole world!* So, He'll respond to my prayers for anyone I pray for. I can see ISIS leaders on a news report and start praying for them. I can say, "Oh, God, I forgive them! Bring laborers across their paths who will tell them about Jesus—and do it quickly, before they get killed. LORD, I surround them with mercy and faith. I loose angels to go whisper in their ears. Give them visions and dreams, LORD, that will draw them to You."

What am I doing when I pray like that? I'm tapping into the anointing. I'm releasing God's delivering, healing power.

God will move on tough-minded politicians in every office of government if someone will pray for them. I'll never forget the first time I really caught hold of that revelation. It was in the 1970s, during a particularly troublesome time in the United States. The president had been making some serious blunders in the war in Southeast Asia, and people by the thousands were being killed. Every time I heard about it on the news, it would make me mad enough at the man to want to fight.

One night, as I was preparing to go preach a meeting, I was tying my tie, just about ready to walk out of the hotel room. For seemingly no reason, I reached over and turned on the television. I never turn on the television before I preach. I didn't even realize I was doing it until it came on and I heard the president's voice. Since I was already praying in preparation for the meeting, while I finished tying my tie, I said out loud, "Heavenly Father, You said to pray for all those in authority so I pray for that man right now in Jesus' Name."

From then on, every time I heard the president's voice, the love of God would just flood my heart. Even though he kept on doing the same kinds of things, instead of getting mad at him, I would pray for him and surround him with love and forgiveness. "LORD, I continue to hold him up to You, Sir," I'd say. "Help him to do what's right in Your sight. Help him!"

After a few months passed, I heard that Billy Graham had spent some time with him. I don't know what they talked about, but I know enough about Billy Graham to be certain that Jesus must have been central to the conversation. A few days after their meeting, the president made the announcement, "I will not be seeking re-election."

I'm sure I wasn't the only believer praying for the president at that time, but God let me be part of turning that man's heart. He let me be part of his forgiveness and of helping God's will to be done, not only in his personal life, but in the life of this nation.

BE SURE TO STAY ON THE RIGHT SIDE OF THE SWORD

While the truth about forgiveness is powerful and thrilling, like everything in The WORD of God, it's also a two-edged sword. It can either work for or against us, depending on what we do with it. If we choose to forgive others, it will work for us and connect us to the same supernatural power that heals, delivers and works miracles. If we refuse or neglect to forgive people, it will work against us because our unforgiveness will choke off the operation of God's Anointing, and His power will be restrained in our lives.

That's dangerous business. We need God's Anointing working for us all the time. We need it working in our families, in our physical bodies, keeping us healed (1 Peter 2:24), and in our finances, empowering us to prosper (Psalm 35:27). We need it to receive answers to our prayers.

Faith, God's Anointing and forgiveness are all tied together. That's why in Mark 11, Jesus said:

> Have faith in God. For verily I say unto you, That whosoever shall say unto this mountain, Be thou

removed, and be thou cast into the sea; and shall not doubt in his heart, but shall believe that those things which he saith shall come to pass; he shall have whatsoever he saith. Therefore I say unto you, What things soever ye desire, when ye pray, believe that ye receive them, and ye shall have them. And when ye stand praying, forgive, if ye have ought against any: that your Father also which is in heaven may forgive you your trespasses (verses 22-25).

Notice Jesus told us to "have faith in God" or, as several translations put it, "have the faith of God" or "the God kind of faith." The God kind of faith is the kind of faith Jesus has. It's the faith in which He functioned when He was on earth—the faith that speaks to mountains and receives whatever it asks for in prayer.

Every one of us who is a born-again believer has what it takes to operate in that kind of faith. Jesus always authorizes and empowers us to do whatever He commands. He commanded us to have the God kind of faith, so that means we can!

That's good news, all by itself. But Jesus didn't stop there. He went on to tell us how to make sure our prayer of faith functions properly. He said, "When you stand praying, forgive." Everything Jesus said about faith hangs on that one command because "faith...worketh by love" (Galatians 5:6), and forgiveness is an essential expression of love. Without forgiveness, faith won't function. It just sits there like a car with a dead battery—going nowhere.

Many Christians don't seem to understand this. They have the idea that forgiveness is optional. "You just don't know what that person did to me!" they say. "I've been trying to forgive him (or her) for years, but I haven't been able to do it. I guess I just need a little more time."

Although such statements might sound reasonable, they directly contradict what Jesus said. He didn't tell us to take years to forgive people. He commanded us to forgive them immediately, while we're praying. He told us to do it before we say amen. Why? Because our faith (and therefore, the *answer* to our prayers) depends on it.

But what if someone has hurt you so badly, you can't even stand the thought of them? What should you do?

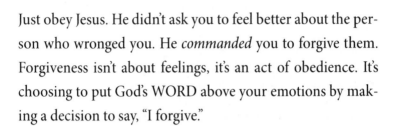

Just obey Jesus. He didn't ask you to feel better about the person who wronged you. He *commanded* you to forgive them. Forgiveness isn't about feelings, it's an act of obedience. It's choosing to put God's WORD above your emotions by making a decision to say, "I forgive."

The quicker you do that, the better off you'll be. By the same token, the longer you wait, the worse things will get and the more deeply mired in unforgiveness you'll become. Remember what I said about how the devil sneaks up on you with offense? He works the same way with unforgiveness. You'll just be going along doing something else entirely when, suddenly, you'll find yourself mentally rehearsing the ugly things someone did and said to you. You'll imagine yourself saying the things you wish you'd said at the time. With each rehearsal, the conversation in your head becomes uglier and the negative effects are re-energized. You'll relive the hurt, and the spirit of division will dig deeper into your thought patterns and inflict more damage.

You might think your thoughts aren't reality, so they can't actually do that much damage, but science has proven otherwise. Thoughts have a very real impact. They can affect not only people's emotions, but their brains and bodies, as well. The most vivid illustration of this reality is seen in the epidemic of pornography. When people view pornography, they aren't engaging in a real act, yet they're experiencing the same results. That's why the devil pushes it. The images and thoughts drive people toward actions that carry disastrous results.

The devil pushes thoughts of unforgiveness for the same reason. Such thoughts put people on a path of destruction. A person might be thinking about a hurtful event or conversation for the second, third, fourth or fifth time, but it's having the same effect it did the first time. It's working on that person's brain and producing all the same toxic reactions. The only difference is, with each repetition, the reactions become worse.

We've all gotten caught in this cycle at one time or another. We've all spent hours, days or even months feeling angry, hurt and upset with someone. It's a miserable experience. But we don't have to stay trapped in it. Instead, we can instantly do what Jesus commanded. As soon as we realize we "have aught against any," while we stand praying, we can forgive.

Even if we don't think we can do it, we must choose by faith to say, "I forgive So-and-So." Thirty minutes later, if you catch yourself thinking about it again, say it again. Don't just think it, say it. If you're around people just whisper, "No, I reject those ugly thoughts. I have forgiven him. I have forgiven her." Every time you do that, the thoughts will stop. They may come back again later, for the first few days, but when they do, they'll be less intense and begin to diminish. Faith words control thoughts.

The person you've forgiven may not have changed at all. They may still be totally in the wrong. But even so, something good will be happening inside *you*. God's Anointing will be flowing. His burden-removing, yoke-destroying power will be working inside you to heal and deliver you from the pain that person caused you. What's more, if the situation is still creating problems, God's powerful Anointing will provide you with the insight you need to solve those problems.

Just think about what a wonderful effect this could have on your family! When Uncle Cranky starts acting ugly toward Aunt Sensitive at the next family get-together, and all the relatives start dividing up and fighting, through releasing forgiveness, you can bring God on the scene. Instead of jumping into the fray with everyone else, you can say, "LORD, I forgive them all."

Then you can bind the devil who's blinded Uncle Cranky's eyes to the gospel and pray for The LORD of the harvest to send laborers across his path so he can get saved.

You don't have to stop with Uncle Cranky, either. This is a wonderful way to live all the time. So, go ahead and make it a lifestyle. Do it constantly, everywhere you go. Every time the spirit of division tries to use people to tear up your life, family, church, neighborhood, city or nation, instead of getting mad at the people and choking off the anointing, pull out the weapon of forgiveness. Release the power of it to go to work in your life and theirs, too. Put the spirit of division on the run by praying for them and saying, "Father, I'm a forgiver, not a condemner. Thank God, I forgive." Then add some more names to your list!

CHAPTER 9

WIMPS, CHAMPIONS, AND TURNING THE OTHER CHEEK

Ye have heard that it hath been said, An eye for an eye, and a tooth for a tooth: but I say unto you, That ye resist not evil: but whosoever shall smite thee on thy right cheek, turn to him the other also.

Matthew 5:38-39

If you're not quite sold yet on the power of forgiveness, I can assure you, I understand. There was a time in my life when I wasn't sold on it, either. As a young man, I ran with a crowd that firmly believed whoever delivered the first punch—either physically or verbally—always won the fight. So for years, I thought the smartest thing to do was to swing first and think later.

Then I got born again and read what Jesus said about turning the other cheek. Initially, I didn't much like it. I thought if I didn't strike back at people, they'd be free to take advantage of me. "LORD, I'm not too keen on this cheek-turning business," I said. So, I went through the New Testament to read about it and was amazed at what I found.

During Jesus' earthly ministry, He consistently turned the other cheek, and yet He still triumphed in every situation. No matter how hard people tried to destroy Him and His ministry, they were never able to succeed.

In Nazareth, for example, the people who came to hear Him preach actually ended up trying to kill Him. They dragged

Him out of the city, took Him up on a cliff and attempted to push Him over the edge. But, they couldn't get the job done. Somehow, Jesus slipped through their fingers, and "passing through the midst of them, He went His way" (Luke 4:30, *New King James Version*).

He did much the same thing one time when He was preaching in Jerusalem and the people got upset about what He was saying. They started picking up rocks to stone Him to death, but instead of fighting, He simply "hid himself" (John 8:59). He walked right by them, cloaked in the power of the Holy Spirit, while they were looking around wondering where He went!

Even in the Garden of Gethsemane, no one could lay a hand on Him until He allowed them to. He made that clear when the band of Roman soldiers came there to arrest Him. They were fully armed, yet all Jesus had to say was, "I am he, [and] they went backward, and fell to the ground" (John 18:6). If that weren't enough to prove who was in charge of the situation, when Peter tried to help out by drawing his sword and cutting off a fellow's ear, Jesus told him to put the sword away. "Thinkest thou that I cannot now pray to my Father, and he shall presently give me more than twelve legions of angels?"

He said. "But how then shall the scriptures be fulfilled, that thus it must be?" (Matthew 26:53-54).

Most people don't even think twice about Jesus doing those things because, after all, He's the Son of God. But the Bible says that you and I are sons of God, too (Romans 8:14-15)! We're Jesus' joint heirs (Romans 8:17), and He said that, as believers, we can do the same works and even greater works than He did (John 14:12). Therefore, if He could live in such a way the devil couldn't get to Him, turn the other cheek, and come out of every confrontation as a victor, we must be able to do that, too!

The devil works hard to keep us from realizing this. He does whatever he can to keep us in fear of what others might do to us, because if we're not afraid, then he's finished. Everything he does is through fear.

The spirit of division is tied to fear. It can't do anything apart from fear. All the bigotry, racism, and demonically driven divisions in the world are fear-based and fear-enforced. Political factions fight each other because one is afraid the other is going to get more power, and they'll lose control. Groups on different rungs of the financial ladder war against each other because one group is afraid they're not going to get what they want, and the other is afraid someone is going to take what they have. Racial tensions erupt because one race is afraid another race is going to deprive them of their rights, oppress them or take advantage of them in some way.

Fear is the source of it all—and the devil is the source of fear.

ORPHANS NO MORE!

Fear is actually faith twisted in the opposite direction. Fear is actually having more faith in the devil and his ability to harm you than you have in God and His love for you and ability to protect you. Just as faith is the spirit connector to God and THE BLESSING, fear is the spirit connector to the devil and the curse.

The first time fear came on the scene was after Adam and his wife sinned in the Garden of Eden: "And The LORD God called unto Adam, and said unto him, Where art thou? And he said, I heard thy voice in the garden, and I was afraid" (Genesis 3:9-10). Why was Adam afraid? Because he'd disrupted his relationship with God. He and his wife had doubted and disobeyed God's WORD, bowed their knee to the devil, and committed spiritual treason. They'd disconnected themselves from their heavenly Father and become spiritual orphans.

The dictionary says an *orphan* is "one without parents or friends." An orphan has no one to whom he can look for protection or provision—no heritage. No one is obligated to him either by blood or by covenant. If anyone takes responsibility to look after him, it's usually because the orphan is a ward of the state.

I grew up at the tail end of the Depression, so I got a revelation early in life of just how scary being an orphan can be. I heard stories about children whose poverty-stricken parents had dumped them off on a doorstep somewhere, and no one even knew who they were. I saw Shirley Temple movies about orphanages run by a big, ugly woman or beady-eyed old man who stole all the food while the kids went hungry. Although today, there are many wonderful Christian orphanages, few such places existed during the Depression. So for the most part, orphans had no one to watch out for them. Spiritually, that's the condition Adam and Eve were in immediately after they sinned. It's also the condition we were all in before we were born again. This is particularly true if we had no

Jewish heritage. We were spiritual orphans in every sense of the word. As Ephesians 2:12 says, we were "without Christ… aliens from the commonwealth of Israel, and strangers from the covenants of promise, having no hope, and without God in the world."

As gentile unbelievers, we didn't qualify for the promises of God given to Abraham and his descendants in the Old Testament. We didn't have any guarantee—covenant—that God would take care of us. People without God develop a culture of self-preservation, fighting for themselves to get ahead so they don't end up getting the short end of any deal. *They* have to look out for No. 1 and don't mind stepping on anyone who might get in the way.

To make matters worse, because of Adam's sin, in addition to being disconnected from God, the Father of love and light, the human race without God was connected to satan, the father of fear and darkness. So, people literally had a fountain of fear flowing inside them all the time.

Now, because of the redemptive work of Jesus, we can all be partakers of the New *Covenant!* Praise God, we're no longer in that situation. We're not spiritual orphans anymore. We've been born into the family of God. We have a faithful, all-powerful heavenly Father who has not "given us the spirit of fear; but of power, and of love, and of a sound mind" (2 Timothy 1:7).

> For ye have not received the spirit of bondage again to fear; but ye have received the Spirit of adoption, whereby we cry, Abba, Father. The Spirit itself beareth witness with our spirit, that we are the children of God: and if children, then heirs; heirs of God, and joint-heirs with Christ (Romans 8:15-17).

We're now living every orphan's dream! We're like the little guy who was sitting in the orphanage thinking no one would ever want him because he was the wrong color, or wasn't smart enough, or wasn't good-looking enough. And then the richest, kindest, most powerful man on earth came in, looked him right in the face and said, "That's my boy, right there! That's the one I want. I'm going to take that child home with me today. I'm going to throw away all his old, tattered clothes and buy him a whole new wardrobe. I'm going to adopt him and make him the heir of everything I have."

Spiritually, that's exactly what happened to us when we believed in Jesus and received Him as our Savior and LORD. Through the new birth, and by a divine covenant of adoption, we became the children of Almighty God! So as God's adopted sons and daughters, everything that belongs to Jesus is ours, as well, throughout all eternity. Every promise God made to Abraham and his descendants now applies to us. "For the promise, that he should be the heir of the world, was not to Abraham, or to his seed, through the law, but through the righteousness of faith" (Romans 4:13).

FIGHT LIKE JESUS DID

With that in mind, if we truly understood who we are and what God has done for us through the New Covenant, we would be the most confident people on earth! Fear and insecurity would be banished from our lives forever. We wouldn't be wasting our time arguing and fighting with other people or allowing the devil to scare us into advancing his agenda of strife and division. Instead, we'd make it our business to *bring people together* in love, and to reign in life as kings (Romans 5:17). We'd be walking around on this planet like we own it because the fact is, we do (Psalm 115:16)!

We not only own it, we've been given the same commission Adam and Eve were given in the beginning when "God blessed them, and…said unto them, Be fruitful, and multiply, and replenish the earth, and subdue it: and have dominion" (Genesis 1:28). We're part of the group God was talking to in Isaiah when He said:

> Hearken to me, ye that follow after righteousness, ye that seek The LORD: look unto the rock whence ye are hewn, and to the hole of the pit whence ye are digged. Look unto Abraham your father, and unto Sarah that bare you: for I called him alone, and blessed him, and increased him. For The LORD shall comfort Zion: he will comfort all her waste places; and he will make her wilderness like Eden, and her desert like the garden of The LORD… (Isaiah 51:1-3).

Notice, according to those verses, Christians not only have a covenant with God, we have an Eden covenant. God has promised to give us days of heaven right here on earth. He's promised to BLESS us so richly that our lives become like the Garden of The LORD.

You may be thinking, *That's wonderful, all right, but I keep running into people who are hell-bent on messing up my Garden. Sometimes it makes me so mad I want to forget about all that cheek-turning stuff and just roll up my sleeves and fight!*

You can fight, but do it like Jesus did when He was on earth. He didn't fight against *people,* He fought against the devil. He fought him by overcoming every temptation to sin, walking continually in love and in God's BLESSING, and bringing that BLESSING into the lives of others. Jesus whipped satan every day of His earthly life, and then finished him off through His crucifixion and resurrection.

The New Testament confirms it time and again:

- He "went about doing good, and healing all that were oppressed of the devil; for God was with him" (Acts 10:38).

- He "spoiled principalities and powers, he made a show of them openly, triumphing over them in it" (Colossians 2:15).

- "Forasmuch then as the children are partakers of flesh and blood, he also himself likewise took part of the same; that through death he might destroy him that had the power of death, that is, the devil; and deliver them who through fear of death were all their lifetime subject to bondage" (Hebrews 2:14-15).

Jesus' final fight with the devil was the most thrilling fight of all time. If you've read about it in the Scriptures, you know how it unfolded. It began with Jesus on the cross and the devil and his crowd thinking they'd finally gotten the upper hand against Him. They didn't know He was there by choice, paying the price for the sin of all mankind, and didn't realize He was acting by faith as our substitute. They thought, somehow, they'd finally overcome Him.

They didn't know they had fallen into the trap of the ages! It was a mystery hidden in God. God put out the bait, and the devil went for it. Jesus "spoiled principalities and powers, he made a show of them openly, triumphing over them in it" (Colossians 2:15). He took the devil's keys of hell and death away from him (Revelation 1:18). He later said to His disciples: "All power is given unto me in heaven and in earth. *Go ye therefore,* and teach all nations, baptizing them in the name of the Father, and of the Son, and of the Holy Ghost: Teaching them to observe all things whatsoever I have commanded you: and, lo, I am with you always, even unto the end of the world" (Matthew 28:18-20). He said, "You go in

My Name and My authority, and I'll be with you."

Let this fact sink into your consciousness: The LORD Jesus Christ is your blood covenant Brother (John 20:17; Romans 8:29; Hebrews 2:11). He utterly defeated the devil in the showdown of the ages. Now, *He has delegated His authority to you.* He has commissioned *you* to enforce His victory by fighting the good fight of faith and keeping the devil under *your* feet.

You might not think you have what it takes to do that, but remember, you've been "born again, not of corruptible seed, but of incorruptible, by The WORD of God, which liveth and abideth for ever" (1 Peter 1:23). First John 4:4 says, "Ye are of God, little children, and have overcome them: because greater is he that is in you, than he that is in the world." Your spiritual DNA and Jesus' DNA are exactly the same. Spiritually, you and He are identical twins. You have the same Father He has. You have the same Holy Spirit inside you. You even have the same faith Jesus has—the very faith of God Himself. It was given to you as a gift the split second you were born again (Ephesians 2:8). The very first time you used it, it changed you forever. It connected you with so much of God's power that your old sinful man died. You became the righteousness of God (2 Corinthians 5:21) and were raised up to sit in heavenly places in Christ Jesus (Ephesians 2:6). And there wasn't one thing satan could do to stop any of it from happening.

Do you understand what this means? It means there's nothing in all of hell or in this world order that your faith in God won't overcome! You *can* overcome the spirits of strife and division and keep their destruction and death out of your home, family, city and nation. When you use your faith in God's WORD like a weapon against the devil, he's helpless against it. "For whatsoever is born of God overcometh the world: and this is the victory that overcometh the world, even our faith" (1 John 5:4). Second Corinthians 10:4 says, "(For the weapons of our warfare are not carnal, but *mighty through God* to the pulling down of strong holds)."

Whether you realize it or not, as a born-again believer, you're the biggest thing on the block to the devil and his crowd! When you stand by faith in God's WORD and refuse to fear, *no one* can overcome you!

One time, a number of years ago, I saw a vivid illustration of this. I was visiting with Dr. E.V. Hill in Los Angeles, and he was driving Gloria and me around some local neighborhoods. At one point, we went through an area that was infamous for violence, and Dr. Hill told us it had been overrun by drug dealers. "They've taken over almost everything except for one particular block that's controlled by a little woman from our church."

I was just about to ask him to tell us about that woman when we turned a corner, and I saw a motherly looking lady who looked to be about 65 years old, standing on the sidewalk with a broom in her hand. "That's her, right there!" said Dr. Hill. "She sweeps that sidewalk every day from corner to corner, praying and declaring The WORD the whole time. You ought to hear her! She sweeps and declares, 'There's no drug dealer comin' on this block! Jesus is LORD over this block!'"

According to Dr. Hill, if any drug dealers did happen to set foot on her sidewalk, instead of cowering in her house she went right out and told them what the rules were. Broom in hand, she'd get right up in their faces and say, "You aren't coming in here peddling none of that demon stuff on my street, in the Name of Jesus. If you want to come here and love God and act right, that's fine. But you bring that dope onto my block, and I'll run you off."

That little woman was so fearless and full of faith, the drug dealers actually thought she was the greatest thing around. Even though she stood up to them, she did it in love and they knew if they ever really wanted to get straightened out, she'd be there to help them.

LIKE A CHAMPION— NOT LIKE A WIMP!

Of course, if you want to operate in that kind of spiritual authority, keeping your foot on the devil's neck in your family, your neighborhood, your city and nation, you can't act like a wimp. You can't go around whining and being afraid someone is going to take advantage of you. Like that little woman in Los Angeles, you have to rise up and live like a champion of faith. How do you do that? You get your Bible and find scriptures that cover your situation. Then, you use them to fight the devil at every turn, just like Jesus did when He backed the devil off on the Mount of Temptation with three powerful words the devil had no defense against. Jesus said, "It is written." (See Matthew 4:1-11; Luke 4:1-14.)

When the devil tries to bring strife and division into your family, your neighborhood, your city or nation, remember what Ephesians 6:12 says: "For we wrestle not against flesh and blood, but against principalities, against powers, against the rulers of the darkness of this world, against spiritual wickedness in high places." So, instead of getting mad at the people the devil's been using to stir things up, find scriptures and use them to build your faith in that area. Think about them. Talk them. Write them down, and put them up everywhere. Fill your house so full of them that when someone comes in, they see those scriptures on every door. Then do what Isaiah 51:1-2 says. Look unto Abraham the father of your faith, and follow his example:

> (As it is written, I have made thee a father of many nations,) before [like] him whom he believed, even God, who quickeneth the dead, and calleth those things which be not as though they were. Who against hope believed in hope, that he might become the father of many nations, according to that which was spoken, So shall thy seed be. And being not weak in faith, he considered not his own body now dead, when he was about an hundred years old, neither yet the deadness of Sarah's womb: He staggered not at the promise

of God through unbelief; but was strong in faith, giving glory to God; and being fully persuaded that, what he had promised, he was able also to perform (Romans 4:17-21).

What do those verses say Abraham was doing? He was using his faith like a craftsman uses a tool—on purpose. Every time the devil called Abraham's attention to his natural circumstances, Abraham hit back with faith. Every time the devil pointed out how impossible it was for God's promise to be fulfilled, he "was strong in faith, giving glory to God; and being fully persuaded that, what he [God] had promised, he was able also to perform."

I'm not suggesting you'll come by this kind of faith easily. You can't do it by staying stuck in an orphan mentality and thinking like a weakling. You have to develop your spiritual muscles by staying in The WORD and standing strongly on it every time the devil challenges you. You have to do what Ephesians 6 says:

Be strong in The LORD, and in the power of his might. Put on the whole armour of God, that ye may be able to stand against the wiles of the devil.... Wherefore take unto you the whole armour of God, that ye may be able to withstand in the evil day, and having done all, to stand. Stand therefore, having your loins girt about with truth, and having on the breastplate of righteousness; and your feet shod with the preparation of the gospel of peace; above all, taking the shield of faith, wherewith ye shall be able to quench all the fiery darts of the wicked. And take the helmet of salvation, and the sword of the Spirit, which is The WORD of God: praying always... (verses 10-11, 13-18).

If you'll follow those instructions, when a fear-filled person comes around trying to mess up your Garden, you'll be able to forgive and love him or her while, at the same time, swinging your WORD sword in the devil's direction until he flees.

He *will* flee because you don't look the same to him as you do to yourself. When you put on your Ephesians 6 war suit, you absolutely terrify him because, after all, it's the full armor *of God!* When you strap on the breastplate of righteousness, take up your shield of faith, and put on the helmet of salvation

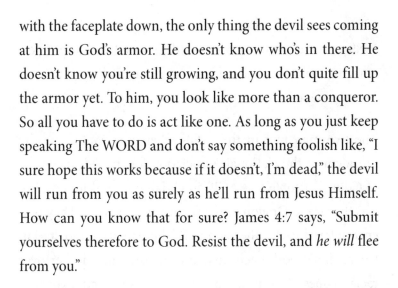

with the faceplate down, the only thing the devil sees coming at him is God's armor. He doesn't know who's in there. He doesn't know you're still growing, and you don't quite fill up the armor yet. To him, you look like more than a conqueror. So all you have to do is act like one. As long as you just keep speaking The WORD and don't say something foolish like, "I sure hope this works because if it doesn't, I'm dead," the devil will run from you as surely as he'll run from Jesus Himself. How can you know that for sure? James 4:7 says, "Submit yourselves therefore to God. Resist the devil, and *he will* flee from you."

Stay in your Bible until your confidence in what God says about it rises up and you become strong in the knowledge of your God-given authority in Him. God sees you as a champion. Get out your faith-preaching CDS and DVDs, and totally immerse yourself in The WORD until your faith is rock-solid, you're fear free and you can stand up to the devil with as much boldness as Reverend Wade Watts did.

WHEN THE NAACP MET THE KKK

Who was Reverend Wade Watts?

He's a wonderful example of a champion of faith. In the 1980s, he met with a man named Johnny Lee Clary. Their amazing story was featured in one of our *Believer's Voice of Victory* magazines.

The two men met in the 1980s when Rev. Watts was the president of the National Association for the Advancement of Colored People (NAACP) in Oklahoma, and Johnny Lee was the Grand Dragon of the state's Ku Klux Klan. They first encountered each other at an Oklahoma City radio station where they'd both been invited to debate one another over racial issues. It was a potentially divisive and explosive situation. Yet, as Johnny Lee tells it, from the outset, Rev. Watts was the picture of kindness. He introduced himself by reaching out to shake Johnny Lee's hand and said, "Hello, Mr. Clary, I just want to tell you I love you, and Jesus loves you."

Caught off guard, Johnny Lee took Rev. Watts' hand…then visibly recoiled at the touch of black skin. "Don't worry, son," Rev. Watts said with a grin. "It doesn't rub off."

Although Johnny Lee was shocked by Rev. Watts' gentility and sense of humor, he didn't let that throw him during the debate. Spewing his racism with a vengeance, he claimed the

Bible commands white people not to mix with black people. He cited studies that supposedly "proved" black children to be less intelligent than white children. He twisted historical facts and argued against the constitutionality of equal rights for all races.

Through it all, Rev. Watts maintained his composure. He refuted Johnny Lee's every argument with kindness and biblical truth until, finally, Johnny Lee erupted in anger. "I'm not going to stay here and listen to any more of this!" he said, storming out of the room.

Later, as Johnny Lee was about to leave the building he saw Rev. Watts holding a baby girl. Lifting up the child, Rev. Watts said to Johnny Lee, "This baby's parents were teenagers. Her mother is white and her daddy is black. The boy's family said they wouldn't have a white child in their home, and the girl's family said they wouldn't have a black child in their home. So I adopted her. Tia is *my* baby now. Mr. Clary, how can you hate this baby?"

Johnny Lee stood speechless for a moment, looking at Tia's lovely little face. Then, clenching his jaw, he turned his back as Rev. Watts words rang in his ears. "You can't do enough to make me hate you, Johnny Lee," he said. "I'm going to love you and pray for you, whether you like it or not."

From that day on, Johnny Lee Clary and the Klansmen harassed and threatened Rev. Watts. For 10 years, they plagued his family with vicious hate-filled phone calls and notes that said, "KKK is watching you." When Rev. Watts joined ranks with an Oklahoma senator to make the Klan's racist hot lines illegal, the group decided to carry out their threats. Johnny was elected to call Rev. Watts with the warning. "We know you're behind this," he said. "We're coming to get you, and we're going to beat you...."

"Hello, Johnny Lee! How's the family?"

"I said we're coming for you!"

"You don't have to come for me, I'll meet you. How about Pete's Place out on Highway 270?"

"Uh..."

"Johnny Lee, they have the best home-cooking you ever tasted—and apple pie that'll make you cry for more. Iced tea in those Mason jars. I can taste it now."

"Did you hear what I said?" Johnny Lee demanded. "We're going to beat you!"

"You be sure and bring all the boys...."

"I said we're going to beat you!"

"I heard you, and that's just fine. But first, I want to buy you boys dinner. Did I tell you about their potatoes?"

Johnny Lee hung up. "What did he say?" the Klan members asked.

"He talked about home-cooking, apple pie and iced tea. Said he wanted to buy our dinner."

"That old man's gone pure crazy," someone said. "Let's leave him alone."

And they did.

For some of the Klansmen, that was the end of the story. But not for Johnny Lee. A few years later, he called Rev. Watts again to say something very different.

"Hello, Johnny Lee," Rev. Watts said warmly when he heard

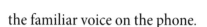

the familiar voice on the phone.

"Rev. Watts, I wanted you to know that I resigned from the KKK in 1989. I gave my heart to Jesus, and I'm a member of an interracial church. My mind is being renewed, and God has called me to preach."

"Well, praise The LORD, son!" Rev. Watts said. "Would you do me the honor of speaking at my church?"

Johnny Lee choked back the tears. "I'd love to."

When Johnny Lee arrived to speak at Rev. Watts' church, there were cameras and news reporters everywhere. Once inside, Johnny Lee Clary stepped up to the podium and looked out over the sea of black faces. The contempt he'd once felt had been replaced with a love so great, so powerful, that his knees felt weak. Remembering how the Klan had professed to be about family and the unity of the white race, he realized unity can never come through fear. Real unity is only possible through love, and an unflinching faith in God and His WORD.

Johnny poured his whole heart into his message that morning. When he finished, a number of people responded and received

Jesus as LORD. Among them was little Tia and three more of Rev. Watts' 13 children—the only members of his family that hadn't yet been born again. As they all hugged each other and celebrated, Johnny Lee Clary and Rev. Wade Watts both knew the love they felt for one another would forever be counted among their greatest treasures. An unbreakable bond of brotherhood had been forged in the fire of a faith strong enough to turn the other cheek.

CHAPTER 10

A SUPERNATURAL SYMPHONY

If two of you on earth agree (harmonize together, make a symphony together) about whatever [anything and everything] they may ask, it will come to pass and be done for them by My Father in heaven.

Matthew 18:19,
The Amplified Bible, Classic Edition

When you consider what happened between Rev. Wade Watts and Johnny Lee Clary, it's easy to see why the spirit of division works so hard to keep believers bound up by fear. When we don't have any fear, we become the devil's worst nightmare because his greatest weapon is fear. We not only move into a place where he can't touch us anymore, we rise up in boldness and operate like Jesus did. We go about doing good and destroying the works of the devil.

Many people think a little fear is healthy, but it's not. The Bible tells us 110 times to *fear not*. God tells us to get rid of fear completely. He doesn't want us to just *manage* fear, control it or cover it up. He wants us to be totally free from it. Every time it rears its ugly head in our lives, He wants us to reject it and declare, "I will not fear!"

The reason The LORD is so adamant about this is because fear connects us to the devil, who is out to steal, kill and destroy us (John 10:10). Fear also causes us to start thinking like spiritual orphans again. It makes us forget that our heavenly Father is "the Father of lights" (James 1:17), and we'll start acting again as if we have to fight our way through the darkness of this world all by ourselves.

Fear puts us in the position spiritually that Gloria found herself in naturally one night a few years ago. She was puttering around the house when, suddenly, all the lights went out. She made her way through the dark and located the lantern I keep in the storeroom. Once she got it turned on, she started looking around at all the stuff in there and spotted an old photo album.

Sitting down on the floor with the lantern beside her, she got interested in looking at pictures. When she finally glanced at her watch, she saw it was time to go to church, so she grabbed the lantern and headed for the bedroom to get ready. As she was walking through the house, lantern aloft, she suddenly burst out laughing. Apparently, while she'd been caught up looking at the photo album, the power had been restored. All the lights in the house were back on again, and she was still walking around carrying that lantern!

When she told me about it later, she pointed out that we as believers sometimes make a similar mistake. We go through life trying to light our own way even though the light of God is shining all around us. Unaware of the fact that He's right there to provide for us and protect us, we fuss and fight and try to fend for ourselves. We live in fear about what's going to happen to us—all because we aren't walking in the revelation of our Father's love for us.

START WITH FAITH, NOT FEELINGS

A revelation of God's love is the ultimate antidote to fear and the strife and division it causes! According to 1 John 4:18, "There is no fear in love; but perfect love casteth out fear.... love turns fear out of doors and expels every trace of terror!" *(King James Version; The Amplified Bible, Classic Edition).* So when we fully know and believe the love God has for us, nothing the devil or anyone else tries to do to us can scare us.

Most people have trouble feeling like God loves them because feelings aren't where the revelation starts. It starts with faith. And, faith comes by hearing and hearing by The WORD of God (Romans 10:17). You believe God loves you the same way you believe every other scriptural truth—by going to The WORD and receiving it by faith. You find out what the Bible says about God's love for you and choose to receive it as truth.

About six years after I was born again, I was studying my Bible in the back bedroom of our tiny, ramshackle house in Oklahoma. I read the prayer Jesus prayed for His disciples in John 17:20-23. Although I'd read it many times before, suddenly, the words leapt out at me in a fresh way:

> Neither pray I for these alone, but for them also which shall believe on me through their word; that they all may be one; as thou, Father, art in me, and I in thee, that they also may be one in us: that the world may believe that thou hast sent me. And the glory which thou gavest me I have given them; that they may be one, even as we are one: I in them, and thou in me, that they may be made perfect in one; and that the world may know that thou hast sent me, and hast loved them, as thou hast loved me.

For a moment, I could hardly believe what I was seeing. Could it possibly be true that God loves me and every other believer as much as He loves Jesus? I looked at it again. Yes, that's clearly what Jesus said.

The realization hit my heart with such force I jumped straight up. "Whew, I believe that! I receive it!" I said. "I confess it as truth right now that God loves me just as much as He loves Jesus!"

Almost instantly, my old religious thinking kicked in, and I thought: *Who do you think you are to stand there in front of God Almighty and say that God loves you as much as He loves Jesus?*

If I'd agreed with those thoughts, they would have talked me out of the revelation of God's love for me before I even caught hold of it. They would have stopped me from believing in His love. And since faith works by love, my faith life would have been crippled. I would have been stuck in that dilapidated house, trying and failing to get ahead for the rest of my life.

But I didn't let that happen. Instead, I believed what the Bible said. I decided that because Jesus said those words in John 17, they *had* to be true, so I could safely agree with them and speak them out loud. I mustered up my courage and declared it again: "Father, Your WORD says You love me as much as You love Jesus.

I know You do because Jesus said so." My knees were shaking a little, but I kept on until I could say it with boldness. I'd take a few steps one way, make my declaration and then, because the room was so small, I'd turn around and take a few steps the other way and say it again. "Praise The LORD, I believe this! I receive it the same way I received my salvation—by faith. I confess this before God: My heavenly Father loves me as much as He loves Jesus!"

I didn't stop when I left that little bedroom, either. I kept on saying it. When I got in my car I'd say, "LORD, I'm going to drive this car today knowing You love me just as much as You love Jesus. I'm going to live this whole day knowing You love me, and You go with me everywhere I go."

After a few days, the Holy Spirit spoke to me again: *Why don't you go back and read the rest of that chapter?*

I hadn't realized it until that moment, but I'd been so thrilled with what I found in verse 23, I hadn't even noticed what Jesus said after that. So I opened my Bible and read the last part of His prayer:

> O righteous Father, the world hath not known thee:
> but I have known thee, and these have known that

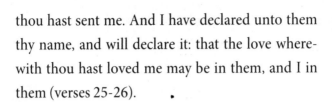

thou hast sent me. And I have declared unto them thy name, and will declare it: that the love where- with thou hast loved me may be in them, and I in them (verses 25-26).

"LORD, it looks to me like those verses are just saying the same thing again," I said. "They're telling me You love me like You love Jesus."

I read it again. Sure enough, when I looked at them again, I saw what The LORD was trying to get across to me. "Glory to God!" I shouted. "Jesus said the love with which God loves Him *is in me!* That means the very love that created this uni- verse—the compassion of God Himself—is living inside me, giving me the power to love like He loves. It means I can love my family, my neighbors, my church and the whole world with God's own love!"

In the years since I received those two revelations, I've discovered how powerful God's love actually is. I've found that as long as I'm believing His love for me and extending that love to others, fear can't get a foothold in me. God's love for me, in me, and working through me, makes fear completely unnecessary. So I can do with it what Gloria did with the lantern that night when

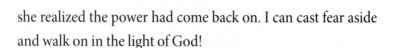

she realized the power had come back on. I can cast fear aside and walk on in the light of God!

NOT A SUGGESTION, A COMMANDMENT

One of the best scriptural descriptions of how all this works is in 1 John 4:16-21:

> We have known and believed the love that God hath to us. God is love; and he that dwelleth in love dwelleth in God, and God in him. Herein is our love made perfect, that we may have boldness in the day of judgment: because as he is, so are we in this world. There is no fear in love; but perfect love casteth out fear: because fear hath torment. He that feareth is not made perfect in love. We love him, because he first loved us. If a man say, I love God, and hateth his brother, he is a liar: for he that loveth not his brother whom he hath seen, how can he love God whom he hath not seen? And this commandment have we from him, That he who loveth God love his brother also.

Notice, that passage is very clear about the responsibility believers have to love each other. It doesn't say God has *suggested* it. It doesn't say He has *recommended* it. It says loving our brother is a *commandment.*

It specifically says that keeping the commandment of love is not hard or "irksome (burdensome, oppressive, or grievous)" (1 John 5:3, *The Amplified Bible, Classic Edition).* It would be if we had to do it in our own strength and emotions, but we don't. We keep God's commandment to love others the same way we receive His love for us—by faith. We do it by taking our stand on The WORD of God and refusing to be moved by contrary feelings.

Personally, I do this first thing every morning. Before I ever leave the house, I set myself up to keep the love commandment by telling Jesus that I love Him, thanking Him for loving me, and acknowledging that His love is in me, empowering me to love others. I begin my day saying things like:

> The love of God is shed abroad in my heart by the
> Holy Ghost (Romans 5:5). I can love even the most
> challenging people, in Jesus' Name. Because God's
> love is in me and His love is patient and kind, I am

patient and kind. I'm not puffed up. I don't envy anyone. I don't lift myself up and put others down. I don't behave in unseemly ways. I'm not selfish and I'm not easily offended. I don't think evil of anyone. I rejoice not in iniquity, but in the truth. God's love *for* me and *in* me enables me to bear all things, believe all things, hope all things and endure all things. Because God's love never fails, my love never fails (1 Corinthians 13:4-8).

Believe me when I tell you, it's better not to wait to make those kinds of declarations until half the day is gone.

Strife and division can crop up before you even realize it, so it's better to commit to walking in love and being a BLESS-ING to *everyone* you encounter before your day begins. Set out in every situation to be a giver and not a taker.

That's the way Jesus is. He gives when times are good and when times are bad. Giving is His lifestyle. He's committed all the time to prospering everyone around Him. Now that sounds easy if you just plan to do it in big things, but doing it in the small events of ordinary life can be a different matter.

Think of the servers in the restaurant where you'll go to lunch, or the people whose job it is to clean the restroom or the checkers in the grocery store, or even the guy who cut you off in traffic. How you act toward those people is important to God.

Did you get mad and say unkind things about the guy in traffic? Did you grab five or six paper towels in the restroom—even though you only needed one—and then carelessly toss them toward the trash container and miss? Did you allow yourself to get irritated with the waitress at the restaurant because she forgot you didn't order gravy on your potatoes? If you're walking in love, you won't act like people's time and effort don't matter. You'll pray for that person who cut you off in traffic, put those extra towels back in the restroom, pick up your towels that missed the trash container and wipe up the water you left on the counter. Instead of being irritated with the waitress, you'll treat her kindly and bless her, even if her attitude may not have been the best toward you. Why? Because Jesus said, "If you've done it for her, you've done it for Me."

DON'T CRITICIZE A MAN'S DIRTY FEET UNTIL YOU'RE READY TO WASH THEM!

The more you develop this mentality and practice obeying the love command, the more integral to your lifestyle walking in love will become. You'll get to the place where the moment you start to say or do something unloving, the Spirit of God will correct you. He'll speak to you and prevent you from reacting to someone in a way you'll later regret.

I remember one time when He did that for me early in my ministry. I was preaching at a church in Fort Worth, and it was just before the morning service. As I stepped out of the pastor's study to walk into the auditorium, the front doors opened and in walked a group of dirty, bare-footed teenagers. There were 13 of them, and they were classic 1960s-style "hippies." They obviously hadn't come anywhere close to soap and water in a long time, so they smelled pretty ripe.

The minute I saw them (and got a whiff of them) something inside me withdrew. I thought, *Where in the world are those kids going to sit?* Right behind the thought came the voice of the Holy Spirit. He spoke to me so loudly I felt the impact of it in every cell of my body. *Don't you criticize a man's dirty feet until you're ready to wash them!*

Those words hit me so hard, it nearly doubled me over. I felt like someone had stuck a hot poker in my heart and the heat of it went all through me. It burned into my inner man.

I went on into the auditorium, and as the kids walked in behind me, I heard whispers ripple through the congregation. One woman said out loud what I had thought earlier, "My God, where are they going to sit?" I realized she needed to hear what I'd just heard so I went to the platform, interrupted the song service, and repeated what God had told me.

His words impacted the congregation the same way they'd impacted me. They set the people's hearts on fire with God's love. It was a moment that changed the church. At the close of the service, when everyone got up to leave, one man called out, "Would everyone just wait a minute? I think before we leave here, we should take up an offering and buy some groceries for these young people. They look hungry to me. Also, I want them to know if they'd like a hot shower or a bed for the night, they can come to my house. If they can wear any of my clothes, they can have them."

Everyone else in the congregation agreed and said, "Yes, that's right. The same goes for me." Men started digging in their pockets and coming up with grocery money. The hippie kids responded, and all of them went home with someone. That night, they all came back to the church for the evening service. As I was preaching, one of them interrupted me. "I just can't wait any longer," he said. "I have to tell you that Jesus Christ is now my LORD!" By the time everything was said and done, every one of those kids was born again. They joined the church, and eight of them eventually entered into full-time ministry!

What made it all possible? When the spirit of division made his play that morning, he lost! When he tried to create hate and separation by magnifying the differences between those young people and the church members, the church rejected him. They kicked him out and chose to walk in love. They let the Holy Spirit take over; He replaced division with reconciliation, and those kids got fed, delivered from drugs, and their lives were changed forever.

Talk about a church rising up and acting like the Church! That's a good picture of it. It's what 2 Corinthians 5:18 is talking about when it says that God "hath reconciled us to himself by Jesus Christ, and hath given to us the ministry of reconciliation."

Reconciliation, not division, is what we as believers are commissioned to bring. Right in the middle of a world that's being torn apart by hate, we're called to bring love. We're commissioned to do the works of Jesus, tell people that He loves them, He's forgiven them, and He wants them to be a part of His family.

As that church in Fort Worth found out that morning, the most effective way for us to fulfill this commission is together. That's why the devil has been so hell-bent on keeping us apart. When we come together, the world sees Jesus in us. When we work and pray together in unity, we operate in the kind of power Jesus told us about in Matthew 18:18-19, when He said: "Whatsoever ye shall bind on earth shall be bound in heaven: and whatsoever ye shall loose on earth shall be loosed in heaven. Again I say unto you, that if two of you shall *agree* on earth as touching any thing that they shall ask, it shall be done for them of my Father which is in heaven."

The word *agree* means "to make a symphony together." It refers to harmonizing with one another like instruments in an orchestra. An orchestra includes many different instruments. It has a piano, but an orchestra is more than just a piano. It has a section of horns, but it also has a string section. When they all play together in harmony with one another, they produce a sound you can't get without all of those instruments playing at once. They make a symphony.

The same is true, spiritually, in the Body of Christ. Each of us is different, yet we're one in the spirit. We don't have to *try* to be one. Jesus has already made us one through what He did on the cross. What we have to do is come together in harmony with each other. When we're in harmony, the power we produce is far greater than the sum of our individual parts. It's so strong that miracles will be done if necessary, in order to carry out what we've agreed on in prayer (Matthew 18:19).

If you're ready for that kind of miracle power in your life, right now just say out loud, "Spirit of division, I'm serving you notice, in the Name of Jesus, my house, my church, my neighborhood, my city are closed to you. I'll not be deceived by you anymore. From now on, I'm not moved by the differences between me and other people. I'm moved by the Spirit of God. My ministry is the ministry of reconciliation. I walk in love because God is love. Whether anyone else loves me or not, is not my business. I'm going to love them because that's what He's told me to do. That's my job, and I'm going to do it!"

Now, get ready for a new day, a new power. Divided, we fall. But once we get together—all heaven will break loose!

Prayer for Salvation and Baptism in the Holy Spirit

Heavenly Father, I come to You in the Name of Jesus. Your Word says, "Whosoever shall call on the name of the Lord shall be saved" (Acts 2:21). I am calling on You. I pray and ask Jesus to come into my heart and be Lord over my life according to Romans 10:9-10: "If thou shalt confess with thy mouth the Lord Jesus, and shalt believe in thine heart that God hath raised him from the dead, thou shalt be saved. For with the heart man believeth unto righteousness; and with the mouth confession is made unto salvation." I do that now. I confess that Jesus is Lord, and I believe in my heart that God raised Him from the dead. I repent of sin. I renounce it. I renounce the devil and everything he stands for. Jesus is my Lord.

I am now reborn! I am a Christian—a child of Almighty God! I am saved! You also said in Your Word, "If ye then, being evil, know how to give good gifts unto your children: HOW MUCH MORE shall your heavenly Father give the Holy Spirit to them that ask him?" (Luke 11:13). I'm also asking You to fill me with the Holy Spirit. Holy Spirit, rise up within me as I praise God. I fully expect to speak with other tongues as You give me the utterance (Acts 2:4). In Jesus' Name. Amen!

Begin to praise God for filling you with the Holy Spirit. Speak those words and syllables you receive—not in your own language, but the language given to you by the Holy Spirit. You have to use your own voice. God will not force you to speak. Don't be concerned with how it sounds. It is a heavenly language!

Continue with the blessing God has given you and pray in the spirit every day.

You are a born-again, Spirit-filled believer. You'll never be the same!

Find a good church that boldly preaches God's Word and obeys it. Become part of a church family who will love and care for you as you love and care for them.

We need to be connected to each other. It increases our strength in God. It's God's plan for us.

Make it a habit to watch the Believer's Voice of Victory Network television broadcast and become a doer of the Word, who is blessed in his doing (James 1:22-25).

About the Author

Kenneth Copeland is co-founder and president of Kenneth Copeland Ministries in Fort Worth, Texas, and best-selling author of books that include *Honor—Walking in Honesty, Truth and Integrity,* and *THE BLESSING of The LORD Makes Rich and He Adds No Sorrow With It.*

Since 1967, Kenneth has been a minister of the gospel of Christ and teacher of God's WORD. He is also the artist on award-winning albums such as his Grammy-nominated *Only the Redeemed, In His Presence, He Is Jehovah, Just a Closer Walk* and *Big Band Gospel.* He also co-stars as the character Wichita Slim in the children's adventure videos *The Gunslinger, Covenant Rider* and the movie *The Treasure of Eagle Mountain,* and as Daniel Lyon in the Commander Kellie and the Superkids™ videos *Armor of Light* and *Judgment: The Trial of Commander Kellie.* Kenneth also co-stars as a Hispanic godfather in the 2009 and 2016 movies *The Rally* and *The Rally 2: Breaking the Curse.*

With the help of offices and staff in the United States, Canada, England, Australia, South Africa, Ukraine, Singapore and Latin America Kenneth is fulfilling his vision to boldly preach the uncompromised WORD of God from the top of this world, to the bottom, and all the way around. His ministry reaches millions of people worldwide through daily and Sunday TV broadcasts, magazines, teaching audios and videos, conventions and campaigns, and the World Wide Web.

Learn more about Kenneth Copeland Ministries by visiting our website at **kcm.org.**

When The LORD first spoke to Kenneth and Gloria Copeland about starting the *Believer's Voice of Victory* magazine...

He said: *This is your seed. Give it to everyone who ever responds to your ministry, and don't ever allow anyone to pay for a subscription!*

For more than 45 years, it has been the joy of Kenneth Copeland Ministries to bring the good news to believers. Readers enjoy teaching from ministers who write from lives of living contact with God, and testimonies from believers experiencing victory through God's Word in their everyday lives.

Today, the *BVOV* magazine is mailed monthly, bringing encouragement and blessing to believers around the world. Many even use it as a ministry tool, passing it on to others who desire to know Jesus and grow in their faith!

Request your FREE subscription to the *Believer's Voice of Victory* magazine today!

Go to **freevictory.com** to subscribe online, or call us at **1-800-600-7395** (U.S. only) or **+1-817-852-6000**.

We're Here for You!®

Your growth in God's Word and your victory in Jesus are at the very center of our hearts. In every way God has equipped us, we will help you deal with the issues facing you, so you can be the **victorious overcomer** He has planned for you to be.

The mission of Kenneth Copeland Ministries is about all of us growing and going together. Our prayer is that you will take full advantage of all The LORD has given us to share with you.

Wherever you are in the world, you can watch the *Believer's Voice of Victory* broadcast on television (check your local listings), the Internet at kcm.org or on our digital Roku channel.

Our website, **kcm.org,** gives you access to every resource we've developed for your victory. And, you can find contact information for our international offices in Africa, Asia, Australia, Canada, Europe, Latin America, Ukraine and our headquarters in the United States.

Each office is staffed with devoted men and women, ready to serve and pray with you. You can contact the worldwide office nearest you for assistance, and you can call us for prayer at our U.S. number, +1-817-852-6000, 24 hours every day!

We encourage you to connect with us often and let us be part of your everyday walk of faith!

Jesus Is LORD!

Kenneth & Gloria Copeland

Kenneth and Gloria Copeland